# COUNTER ATTACK

# COUNTER ATTACK

*Published in aid of Racing Welfare and Rehabilitation of Racehorses*

Published in 2002 by Raceform Ltd
Compton, Newbury, Berkshire, RG20 6NL
Raceform Ltd is a wholly owned subsidiary of MGN Ltd

Copyright © Raceform 2002

A catalogue record for this book is available from the British Library.

ISBN 1-901100-49-9

Edited by Chris Cook
Designed by Sam Pentin
Printed and bound by The Gresham Press, Old Woking, Surrey

# CONTENTS

**Foreword**
– Tony Stafford ..................................................................................................8

**Introduction**
– Prince Rajsinh Rajpipla ('Pippy') ..........................................................9

**'Value'**
– Tom Segal, Mark Coton & Dave Nevison ...............................................11

**Betting Psychology**
– Pippy, Paul Haigh & Kate Fox ...............................................................16

**The View from Behind the Counter**
– David Hood (William Hill), Mike Dillon (Ladbrokes), Jeremy Scott (Tote),
Victor Chandler & Simon Clare (Coral) ....................................................22

**Reading the Market**
– Pippy, Barry Dennis, Andy Smith & Gary Wiltshire ...............................30

**Choosing How to Bet**
– Nick Fox....................................................................................................38

**At the Track**
– Simon Holt, Gerald Delamere, Alan Amies & Richard Austen .................42

**In the Shops**
– John McCririck...........................................................................................50

**Inside Information**
– Pippy, Ivor Herbert, John Sexton & Michael Church ...............................53

**Flat or Jumps?**
– Chris McGrath & Pippy..............................................................................59

**Taking a Fresh Approach**
– John Whitley, Graham Wheldon, Craig Thake, Paul Jones, Mark Howard,
Ken Hussey, Dave Bellingham, Marten Julian & Jim McGrath ..................78

**Betting at Short Prices**
– Pippy .........................................................................................................95

**The Pros**
– Henry Rix, Alan Potts, Eddie Fremantle & Mark Nelson .......................100

**Gamblers' Tales**
– John Oaksey, David Ashforth, Laura Thompson, Mike Cattermole,
Sir Clement Freud, Tony Morris, Tony Stafford, Ian Carnaby
& Julian Wilson ........................................................................................108

**Tote Betting**
– Peter Jones, Pippy ..................................................................................126

# Rehabilitation of Racehorses

Launched by the BHB in April 2000, Rehabilitation of Racehorses is a registered charity aimed at supporting the reschooling and re-homing of former racehorses.

Around 4,000 horses leave Racing every year. With the right expertise and facilities, ex-racehorses adapt well to other equine activities such as showjumping, eventing, polo, dressage and hacking. Unfortunately, things do not always work out as planned and each year the existing rehabilitation centres are asked to take in up to 200 horses in total.

Racing has accepted that it has a responsibility towards these horses and, accordingly, all sectors of the industry are now contributing towards the fund. With a lot of goodwill on all sides, we have reached our initial targets, but there is no room for complacency.

The current policy of the Trustees is to allocate grants to established well-regarded rehabilitation centres that already enjoy charitable status and are financially sound. The Trustees have committed a set minimum sum for the next three years to each of the three centres currently supported: the Thoroughbred Rehabilitation Centre in Lancashire, Greatwood in Devon and the Moorcroft Racehorse Welfare Centre in Sussex.

The intention is to increase that level of support, giving the centres the funds to increase the number of horses taken in and, for the long term, we are examining the option of establishing a new centre to be run by the charity itself.

*Annie Dodd,*
*Rehabilitation of Racehorses,*
*42 Portman Square,*
*London W1H 6EN.*
*Tel: 0207 343 3309.*

# RACING  WELFARE

Racing Welfare is a new organisation formed on 1 January 2001 by the amalgamation of the Racing Welfare Charities, the Stable Lads Welfare Trust and the Jockey Club Charitable Trust.

It can provide help and support to anyone who is working or has worked in the horseracing or thoroughbred breeding industries. In fact, virtually all our assistance goes to stud and stable staff, as, of course, jockeys in need are usually supported by the Injured Jockeys Fund. Nevertheless, we do liaise with them regularly to ensure that, whenever help is needed, it is available.

The new combined charity has the size to be significant. We have some 250 permanent beneficiaries and assist financially another 250 or so each year on a temporary basis.

We also help many others with practical assistance and advice, most often to ensure that they receive the statutory benefits that they are due. In addition, we provide ongoing support for a small number of people seriously handicapped through accident or illness. We own over 100 homes for working and retired staff, including some with warden and nursing care on-site.

*Racing Welfare,*
*20B Park Lane,*
*Newmarket,*
*Suffolk CB8 8QD.*
*Tel: 01638 560 763.*

*All royalties from the sale of this book will be divided between Rehabilitation of Racehorses and Racing Welfare.*

# FOREWORD

BACK in the early 1970s, I was part-time editor for *The Racehorse*, a long-mourned magazine published by Raceform. We had an unusual French correspondent in those days, none other than Prince Rajsinh of Rajpipla.

Pippy, as he prefers to be known, has several rare distinctions, not least that his late father, the Maharajah, won the Epsom Derby with Windsor Lad. As a racing observer, he first made his mark in England, where he owned a number of good horses in the Peter Cazalet stable, indeed selling the winner of the Windsor Centenary Chase to Queen Elizabeth the Queen Mother.

While he was in France, it was my pleasure to receive his hand-written weekly bulletins, in which he showed a deep understanding of racing in the Paris region and, more importantly, the key personalities.

When taxed with the responsibility of finding an alternative source of jumping talent to the much-inflated Irish market of the time for the Dickinson family, he offered two horses. Flying Hugue, the younger, landed a first-time gamble at Catterick. The other, French Hollow, had been a high-class Flat-racer for owner Malcolm Parrish, and under the expert Tony, Monica and Michael Dickinson tuition became a top hurdler here before finishing his career in the United States.

One Monday morning, Pippy showed his mettle. The previous day, Youth had won the Prix Lupin for owner Nelson Bunker Hunt and trainer Maurice Zilber. Lester Piggott, meanwhile, was third on stable-neglected Empery.

Pippy was close by as Lester told the trainer: 'I'll ride him at Epsom'. Pippy said: 'We'll have to back him for the Derby, you know.' That 33-1 proved the bet of most people's lifetimes, and, as Empery fulfilled the script easily at Epsom, Pippy's own stock could not have been higher among *The Racehorse*'s readership.

The quality I admire most in an increasingly suffocating world of received opinion is that of individuality. He forms his own opinions and conclusions and has consistently profited from them.

*Tony Stafford*
*Hertfordshire,*
*May 2002*

# INTRODUCTION

THE late Hollywood mogul Samuel Goldwyn decreed that 'Nothing succeeds like excess'. He must surely have been reincarnated by the BHB to devise the current fixture list. In 2002, this overladen and unrelenting programme has become the bookmakers' not-so-secret weapon, posing punters the questions; Where to bet? When to start? When to stop?

Though hosted by charming and ever-helpful staff, the betting shop mounts an onslaught upon one's powers of resolve and concentration, hell's kitchen with more temptation than could be found in the Garden of Eden. Restraint, self-discipline and patience are imperative to keep you afloat in a punting ocean which can all too often resemble the Red Sea.

An intensive and varied menu of smorgasbord proportions is on offer to satisfy your gambling appetite, but no-one is ordering you to bet and time is on your side. Throw caution to the wind and you will become history but without its historical kudos. On the plus side, 'betting shop widows' can rest assured that their lesser halves will have no time for infidelity and are odds-on to return to the nest, although the egg might have been blown.

However, thanks to the kindness and support of all the contributors who have donated their time and expertise to make this book happen, I am more than hopeful that their comments and advice, based upon their success and experience, will swing the odds in your favour.

Readers of my book *The War Zone* (published in 1998) will already be familiar with some of my advice, though this has, of course, been updated for the post-tax era.

I hope you enjoy this book and that, next time you visit the bookie's shop, you'll be well-prepared for a successful counter attack.

*Prince Rajsinh Rajpipla ('Pippy')*
*London, May 2002*

# CHAPTER 1
# 'VALUE'

Having worked on the Racing Post for some years, **TOM SEGAL** took over the hugely influential 'Pricewise' column, which has for years been an excellent guide to big-priced winners in competitive handicaps, in the summer of 2001. His notable 'Pricewise' successes have included That Man Again (33-1 into 5-1) and Marsad (22-1 into 11-2).

## How Important is Value When Having a Bet?

WELL, that depends on a whole host of factors but the most important, without a doubt, is the temperament of the person parting with the cash.

Take cricket, for example. Mike Atherton and Geoffrey Boycott are short-priced favourite-backers. They take no risks and have solid techniques, so are just as likely to win in the long run as the Graham Thorpes or Ian Bothams of this world.

However, we'd all pay to watch the latter pair, who provide a bit of excitement and colour to the whole proceedings. They wouldn't be messing about with 6-4 shots - they be prepared to have a go, try something different. They're the match-winners, they do the things we all remember and they're the ones that provide all the entertainment.

They may not have the strike-rate or the average of the plodders but, like cricket, betting is designed to bring about excitement and a few big-priced winners is worth much more than five short-priced ones. Thorpe and Botham would be much more interested in the concept of value, because they're risk takers.

Clearly, there's no guarantee of winning whichever way you chose and one way is not better than the other, but fun is what it's all about and why we all started betting, so those boring old sods that tell you to be selective, nick a half a point here or there and keep a record of every bet are missing the point.

Do we really care if we get 11-4 or 3-1 about a 5-2 shot? The answer, unless you're J P McManus and betting in hundreds of thousands of pounds, is no. Do we care if we get 20-1 about a horse that has a 10-1 chance of winning? Of course we do and that is basically all that value betting is.

It's not very scientific and you don't have to work for NASA to work it out but, if you keep getting a bigger price than truly represents your horse's chance in any given race, then your chances of winning in the long run are greatly enhanced.

Here's the catch. Why is there always a catch?

Getting the value doesn't guarantee winning and this is where the temperament factor comes in, because the one thing you have to put up with when backing horses at bigger prices is long losing runs and plenty of people can't cope with that.

If you hide behind the sofa when you've got a tenner on a 10-1 shot, then value betting is not for you, but, if you work hard enough and keep thinking about the sport and watching horse races, then there will be plenty of horses priced at much bigger odds than reflect their chance of winning.

If you keep your chin up and keep confidence in your methods, then a lot of those horses will win and you'll begin to feel a bit like a Thorpe or a Botham and there can be nothing better than smashing Shane Warne for six at Lords, or bagging a couple of double–figure priced winners in quick succession.

It doesn't take too many of either to make a big difference.

---

As a writer for the Racing Post in the 1980s, **MARK COTON** founded the 'Pricewise' column and immediately got it off to a flyer – his first three tips won at double-figure prices and the most influential tipping column of its time was born. He is the author of two books on gambling and is Racing Editor of Raceform On Saturday.

## Why Value Isn't Worth It

LET'S begin with a piece of dialogue from a recent TV racing programme.

'Well, Robert, to sum up, there are a couple of interesting 12-1 shots in this field, but I'll stick with value and go for the 5-4 favourite.'

Sorry for taking liberties, but the dialogue is pure invention. And the fact that it is almost inconceivable such an argument would be raised in this or any other forum reveals a profound limitation in the concept of value. Theoretically, the argument is plausible, for it is just as likely, if not far more so, that the average 5-4 favourite will represent value over a 12-1 shot. That's the problem with value, it's too theoretical.

If you're smart with figures, have sharp trading skills and abundant spare hours at your disposal, then value might be the approach for you, built around a compilation of your own tissue to compare with prices on offer in the marketplace, but most of us don't want betting to be this complicated.

Only in the 'Pricewise' column in the *Racing Post* has value successfully reached a wide audience and even here it has operated within very narrow parameters, namely the big handicaps and leading conditions races.

So what of an alternative?

Perhaps we should begin by asking ourselves what we want from our betting. The response isn't necessarily as obvious as it might initially seem; beyond the money, there is the urge for a sense of involvement, of anticipation constantly renewed, a chance to exercise skill and judgement without working as hard as, well, a professional. The most elusive quality in this game is confidence. How hard it is not to get caught in betting's Catch 22. You can win only if you're confident. And how to develop confidence? You need to win.

Or to seek winners. At a high strike-rate.

In the age of value, it was all too easy to turn our noses up at short-priced favourites, even winners, like wine snobs, as if it wasn't worth our time getting involved in them.

What misguided souls we were.

In a high percentage of races, the favourite is the key horse. You need to get a line on whether it is potential betting material, ought to be opposed, or if it's too hard to judge either way. Far too often, a value temptation drew us away from this key task in favour of idle speculation about horses at bigger prices.

Perhaps the most telling indication of the limitations of value has been that the big bookmakers were never in the least afraid of it and not only because it encouraged a wide audience to become enamoured with competitive races (interestingly, often sponsored by the bookies themselves). A quick price-cut here and a knock-back there easily kept liabilities within bounds.

So what of a formula for the ideal we envisage?

Firstly, develop a method and, once you know the method has power, place absolute trust in it. Never allow a selection filtered through your method to be trumped by one from another.

It needn't be complicated. A gambler friend of mine likes topweights in nurseries, horses carrying a penalty in races of similar quality to the one they've just won, and the top trainer at the track. It takes him around fifteen minutes to mark off his selections in the cafe in the morning and he backs more winners than the average value devotee dare even dream about.

The professionals are right when they speak of the importance of thinking against the grain and there is plenty of mileage left in this idea.

We're constantly being told by the bookmakers and the media to concentrate on races with big fields, so maybe we should start studying small ones. Many moan about the quality of racing, finding it all too harrassing, so perhaps we might zero in on the worst races rather than the best ones.

And most of all, it is surely high time to turn our backs on the concept which started as an experimental alternative and has become an orthodoxy, namely value itself.

**DAVE NEVISON** *was a worker in the City of London before boredom drove him out to become a professional gambler in the early 1990s. Between trips to Southwell and Lingfield, he finds time to write weekly columns in the* Racing & Football Outlook *and the* Daily Record.

## *Ladies Prefer Value-Seekers*

THE concept of 'value' in betting seemed to hit the streets in the mid-1980s and, since then, has probably become the most widely-used term in any discussion about betting at any level. It certainly seems to have overtaken 'winner' in most punters' perception of what is the most important aspect of a bet, which is at first surprising but, when taken to its natural conclusion, is perhaps not such a shock.

As a value-seeking punter you are revered and admired by your contemporaries, much more so than if you are simply someone who picks a lot of winners. To be labelled a 'favourite backer' is the pits among the punting cognoscenti.

This state of affairs is never more obvious than when watching the pundits on the Racing Channel as they run through their morning selections. The expression on Alex Hammond's face when the guest puts up a bet that isn't the favourite is a joy to behold. 'Going for a bit of value are we, big boy?' is what I imagine she's thinking, while hastily scribbling down her hotel room number for after the show!

Protocol dictates that such things don't happen, but pundits who consistently put up favourites, even winning ones, do not get anywhere near the same response from the glamorous presenter. The ability to sort out the 'value' lifts you above most punters, even if you invariably end up skint.

The value punter, apart from being a more sexually attractive being, also has the one thing all punters need more than anything; a ready-made excuse that deflects from his own failings and confirms to himself that he is not actually a loser but a winner waiting to happen.

How often have we sat in the pub, betting shop or racetrack and watched the short-priced favourite gag up just as we expected it would. To share in the victory, we turn around to our friends and point out that we could easily have backed that one but instead decided to go for the' value' bet at bigger odds. As we turn around to take the applause from our colleagues, we see the 'value' trotting home about a furlong behind the others, while, in the foreground, all the losers are collecting their winnings on the good thing.

I don't believe there are too many punters who have not been in this situation and it is all because we have become obsessed with getting the value rather than getting the money. Even the top newspaper columnists have caught this disease.

I have lost count of the number of times the 'Pricewise' column in the *Post* tells us that he thinks the favourite will win but his credibility would go out of the window if he tipped it. Instead, he puts up some aged cripple who has the beating of the jolly on one run three years ago in an auction plate! Needless to say, the bet, in these circumstances, is always the jolly.

To conclude, value is a marvellous thing but you cannot eat it. I hate to end this piece praising Derek Thompson but just about the only time he has said anything useful on Channel Four was when he interrupted his guest and told him to forget about the value and just 'tell us the winner.'

A lot of value bets end up in the rubbish bin.

# CHAPTER 2
# BETTING PSYCHOLOGY

IN the pre-betting shop era, most of the leading course layers were operating with their own money. To an extent, this put them in a similar position to their biggest punters.

On a losing run, thanks to a string of fancied winners, bookmakers tended to extend odds in an attempt to recoup losses by seducing backers to play up their winnings. That was when 'value' really became evident.

However, if they were doing well and the positions were reversed, they would close ranks and tighten up prices, secure in the knowledge that all but the patient and experienced player would accept under the odds, trying to get out of trouble.

This produced a straight fight – punter versus bookmaker.

Today, the major quartet of bookmakers can afford to sit back, take bets, take stock of every situation and wait for us to make mistakes. Therefore, we must in turn watch and wait for one or more of them to err on the side of generosity and take advantage of it. The average punter on an all-too-frequent losing run is pressurised into error and suffers accordingly. Time and weight of capital are on the shop's side, as is the potent advantage of being able to shorten prices to cut losses.

You can counteract by wagering within your limits, exercising patience and restraint. Off-course layers and the shop can recover three months' losses in three good weeks – the punter can give back winnings in treble-quick time. Make no mistake; on a losing run, punters can make more unforced errors than the bookmakers are likely to.

Treat each day as it comes, don't play up your winnings, don't become one of the shop's perennial favourites. Keep a level head and, if you're satisfied with your annual results, don't change your tactics.

Let's say that, with everything in your favour, you've drawn up your betting plan and entered the fray but the horse or horses fail to deliver. What should you do? Retreat! You may be financially wounded but you won't be psychologically scarred (a condition which, when it affects a punter, operates to the benefit of the bookies).

If you lose, don't chase – stop, take stock and analyse what went wrong. Try to profit from this setback with your newly-gained knowledge.

This is a situation in which attack is not the best form of defence. It's both stupid and irresponsible to go after your lost stake with 'second liners'. Double trouble could well ensue, leaving you with little or no ammunition for your next sortie when, if following your chosen format, you'll have a much better winning chance than if charging in blindly.

If you stick to this approach, you'll have no regrets when things turn against you. Losing when you're out of control will leave you needing more than a bit of luck to break even.

There's a world of difference between being out of luck and being out of form.

When you're out of luck, photo-finish verdicts go against you. Your tried and trusted jockey makes a rare error of judgement, your horse meets with ill luck in running or your good thing blunders its chance away at the final flight with the race at its mercy.

At such times, console yourself with the thought that you're still in the right groove. Keep punting until you go out of form.

You'll know when that happens – your selections just never seem to be troubling the judge. Either your judgement has become impaired or you're betting at a time when the results strongly favour the bookies.

This is the time to sit it out and assess the racing you see without the burden of financial involvement. Wait until you think results are starting to favour the way you bet once again.

As so often happens, the horses you would have backed will sometimes win. When they do, you'll go to hell and back but at least you won't be paying for the return ticket. At such times, you're at your most vulnerable, liable to fall for tips which would be noted but not supported at other times. Hold firm – you'll eventually be back on the road to punting recovery.

If you're looking for further insight into your thoughts and those of your fellow gamblers, then who better to ask than highly-experienced punter Paul Haigh and racing's anthropologist Kate Fox?

 **PAUL HAIGH** *has been producing several weekly columns for the* Racing Post *since the mid-1980s, while also finding time to contribute to* The Guardian, The Times, The Daily Telegraph, The Daily Express, The Daily Mail *and various magazines. He has previously written or contributed to four books.*

## The Outlook on Life That Makes Us Best

THE psychology of the punter is a riddle wrapped in an enigma, marinaded in mystery and carefully sealed in several layers of tinfoil.

It is nothing that the average person, obsessed as he or she is by such foolishness as ISAs and TESSAs and pension plans and the general paraphernalia of economic prudence, can possibly relate to. And, as is usual with mindsets that are beyond the comprehension of the average person, it tends therefore to be dismissed as an aberration at best, as a form of disgraceful irresponsibility at second best, and at worst as a form of mental illness.

That's OK, sad people. We don't think much of you either. It was Michael Stoute who told me once that, when he was just a kid starting out, a wise old man took him aside and gave him what he still regards as some of the best advice he's ever received.

'Unless you absolutely can't help it' intoned the grizzled sage 'never under any circumstances have anything to do with anyone who isn't interested in racing.'

For 'racing' substitute 'betting' in that wonderfully shrewd suggestion, and you're left with a pretty serviceable code of behaviour for those of us who simply cannot comprehend the sort of tedium that has to be endured by all those unfortunates who have chosen – CHOSEN, mind you – to deny themselves the multifarious joys of the punt.

Frankly, I think they're all quite beyond the pale. But because they're always so generous with their self-righteousness, their 'sensible' prescriptions and their infuriating tut-tutting (have you noticed how all these deadbeats expect you to buy a round of drinks when you've had a winner, then order themselves a double, and tell you it's a mug's game when you haven't?), here is one last attempt to explain to the have-nots, not how our brains work, because that would be much too complicated for them, but just what it is that drives us on.

Punters believe they are cleverer than the average drone. If they didn't, then (fairly obviously) they wouldn't punt. In particular, they believe they are cleverer than bookmakers, spread-makers and, it goes almost without saying, all the rest of the people who use the Tote. Theirs is a glorious intellectual arrogance and one entirely impervious to the feeble weaponry that can be brought to bear on it by experience.

Bust a punter one day and fair enough, yes, he will swear off that evening. And forever more. Next day, however, he will wake mentally refreshed and with hope renewed. He will look at the paper, see who's running and have no less unshakable opinions than he had the morning before about the likely outcome of races – or about the economic imperative that he get hold of another bankroll and stick it on forthwith.

Now that's what I call resilience. Arctic explorers? SAS men? Rugby league forwards? Forget 'em. Punters are the toughest nuts you'll ever meet.

Punters are also the greatest optimists on earth. Which is one reason why they're such damnably attractive people. If you want pessimists, go to banks. Or insurance offices. Fancy the really gloomy types? Don't bother with undertakers. Just surround yourself with chartered accountants.

Punters aren't plodders. They always believe they're just one step, just one good day, away from triumph. And their lives – our lives I mean, of course – are things of pleasure and beauty in consequence.

Punters know their own minds. They know they're right and their failures are never their . . .

Good grief, did you see the ride that moron gave the favourite? Ever considered a lobotomy, you bastard? Did I tell you how close I was to getting the trifecta up in last year's Cambridgeshire? And I would have done, too, if it hadn't been for . . .

Oh never mind, never mind. Sad bugger like you. You wouldn't understand.

**KATE FOX**, *a social anthropologist, is co-Director of the Social Issues Research Centre in Oxford and has researched and written about many aspects of human behaviour. In 1996 she was commissioned by the British Horseracing Board to conduct research on racegoers; the result was her popular book* The Racing Tribe *(Metro Publishing Ltd).*

## Racecourse Gambling – an Anthropologist's Perspective

PEOPLE are attracted to racing for many reasons other than gambling. About 30% of racegoers, the ones I call 'Socials', are not even there for the racing, but to engage in various forms of social bonding. Even among Enthusiasts, gambling is only one of the attractions.

Racing has a unique atmosphere. It has its own social micro-climate, characterised by a highly unusual combination of relaxed inhibitions and exceptionally good manners. This is extremely rare: if you think about it, you normally get either one or the other. Either people are shedding their inhibitions and letting their hair down, or they are being frightfully polite and well-behaved. At the races, they somehow manage to do both at the same time.

Most people at race meetings are betting 'for fun', usually in quite small amounts (average bet £2.50), so it's not really about making money. People are attracted to betting not just by the prospect of winning, but because we all have a deep-seated need for risk-taking. This urge to take risks is hard-wired into the human brain; it is part of our evolutionary heritage.

Our ancestors experimented with fire, explored unknown territory and tried to ride wild horses. Nowadays, our lives are much less risky, but the wiring is still there, we still need the excitement and adrenaline rush of risk-taking – and we can get this from betting a few quid on a horse.

The bonding effect of shared risk-taking is also available at the races. Any form of shared risk-taking tends to bring people closer, to promote greater intimacy. This is why companies send their employees rock-climbing and canoeing as a 'team-building' exercise. People who have backed the same horse have an instant bond: they call it 'our horse'.

And the bonding effect works even with people who have backed different horses: you get a sort of friendly rivalry, lots of banter and debate.

Then, there's the 'us and them' factor. This bonding effect I've described is further enhanced at the races by the feeling that punters are engaged in a collective battle against the bookies.

Although bookies and punters are essentially engaged in the same enterprise – trying to make a profit out of predicting the outcome of races – it is the bookie who is characterised as greedy and sinful, while the innocent punter is 'fleeced', like a sacrificial lamb.

Bookies perform a social function which is, in some respects, similar to that of the medieval 'sin-eaters' – a person hired at funerals to take upon himself the sins of the deceased person, through the ritual consumption of a crust of bread and ale, thus allowing the soul of the departed to be delivered from purgatory.

So successful has been the transfer of sin to this marginalized caste that punters can speak proudly of 'beating the bookies' or 'outsmarting the bookies', as though they were knights in shining armour doing battle against the forces of darkness.

Finally, here's a note on betting etiquette as I've observed it.

In the unwritten etiquette of betting at race-meetings, £2 is a 'lady's bet' and anything below a fiver casts serious doubt on the masculinity of the punter. The rule for males is: either don't bet on a race at all, or bet at least £5. Even males who are complete novices seem to pick up on this unspoken rule very quickly.

Male Suits (corporate racegoers) are the only exception to this rule: if you see a man placing a £2 bet at the Tote counter, the chances are that he is with a corporate party. This is because corporate racegoers tend to bet almost exclusively with the Tote, and the Ladies in Red are far too polite to express any disapproval of effeminate bets, so Suits are less likely to become aware of their error. The only other exception I came across was one that proved the rule: a particularly tight-fisted male who enlisted his female companions to put bets on for him!

It's important to note, however, that although (non-Suit) males must bet at least £5, there is little kudos to be gained by betting much more. Macho status does not increase exponentially in line with larger bets.

A bet of £5 or £10 is quite respectable in most circles and, although there are some very heavy gamblers at racecourses, they are a small minority and there is no need to imitate them.

# CHAPTER 3
# THE VIEW FROM BEHIND THE COUNTER

EVEN if bookmakers and the Tote knew the percentage of annual winners among their regular customers, they would be reluctant to disclose the figure, for fear of disillusioning their clients.

However, if they could and did, their turnover would not suffer, such is the compulsion and optimism of the average betting shop punter. The most devout habitues of such places arrive before the first and, like the Olympic flame, don't go out until the final heat has been decided.

We couldn't get the bookies to tell us how many punters they regularly have to pay out to, but they were happy to offer some other insights.

**DAVID HOOD**
*William Hill*

THE lot of the Odds Compiler is not necessarily a happy one.

A cross-breed between mathematician and form student, they're closeted away with the unenviable task of having to try and please everyone. For their employers, they must be biggest price about the losers and shortest price the winners and, of course, quite the opposite for the punter!

Then there's the racecourse PR representative to contend with. Eager to snatch the tabloid headline or TV quote, the compiler must, in about 20 seconds flat, be able to analyse a race and offer some ludicrous ante-post price for next year's Classics (still eight months away) and yet balance the books when the day of reckoning comes round. The guesswork may have become a little easier in recent years, with the inevitable exchange of loose-leaf formbook for the luxury of a computer mouse. But it's still all about opinions and this is what makes the fight between bookmaker and punter one of the most dangerous battlefields to play in.

You see, it's not all maths. Try second guessing every devious handicapping ploy of the trainers, owners, punters and, of course, the four-legged creatures themselves. The sheer levels of detective work engaged by an odds compiler and his on-course rep would be sufficient to pass any entry-level exam for Scotland Yard.

And then there are the day-to-day imponderable factors that makes this big boys' game so intriguing.

Of course, in hindsight, the clues are always there . . . it's just a case of recognizing them beforehand. A change in riding plans, a new trip, a change from a left-handed to a right-handed track, is it flat or undulating, where are the stalls placed?

All these things have to be taken into account, weighed up and their relevance measured. And, as if that's not hard enough, you've got to second-guess the jolly old weather man as well! The ground is possibly the most crucial factor of all. Will it rain? How much will it rain? When will it rain? Will it get in to the ground? Oh, to have a crystal ball!

Once everything has been considered, the odds tend to be governed by the apparent probability of a horse's chance of success, with bookmakers pricing up all horses to a theoretical over-round percentage. If a compiler considers a horse to have an exceptional chance, perhaps an Even money chance, he is allocating it a value equivalent to 50% of his total book.

The next best, in his opinion may be a 3-1 chance, which takes up another 25% of his book and maybe the next is a 9-1 chance, which eats up another 10%, and so on, until he's finished.

At this point he may find himself, depending on the type of race (maidens and handicaps etc) betting to a nice over-round (anything over 100%), say 120%, which gives him a theoretical profit margin of 20%.

But that's all theory, and dependent on every horse in the race being equally backed, so that the bookmaker's over-round works out. But, as is more often the case, it's only the favourites that get backed and you can't give away the outsiders.

And so to the latest spectre that hangs above the bookmaker's head; the newspaper/professional tipster! Depending on their influence, they're capable of creating an enormous imbalance of support for certain horses and thus make it impossible to actually 'make a book'.

A book often ends up 'over-broke' (horses backed to less than 100%), meaning the bookmaker doesn't always win.

Honest!

**MIKE DILLON**
*Ladbrokes*

WE'VE had lots of practice at pricing up races and we usually find these days that the market falls into place fairly quickly.

For us, the process starts with our ante-post expert John Thomson, who's been assessing races for Ladbrokes for over 20 years now. He's an excellent judge of form and, as soon as we get the five-day entries for any race, he uses his familiarity with the horses to price them up.

In that sense, there's not a lot of difference between us and any punter – we both start by using experience to weigh up the form on offer.

Of course, in these days of internet databases and computerised handicapping, there are all sorts of aids available to those analysing a horserace. In my view, punters have never been better informed than they are now.

There are so many dedicated publications, offering insights into every race, and I believe that trainers are more and more willing to talk frankly to the press about their runners. You still get some cagey types but, by and large, trainers appreciate the need to promote the sport and keep the public well-informed.

Like punters, we're perfectly prepared to take a view about a horse. We're not especially concerned about the prices on offer from other bookies – if we settle on a price for a horse, we'll stick to it, even if it turns out to be bigger than anyone else.

For example, I was at Newbury in March to watch Moor Lane, who was then the ante-post favourite for the Grand National. Frankly, I wasn't impressed and pushed our price out to 16s from 12s straight after his race.

The other High Street bookies stayed at about 10-1, but our judgement was vindicated when Moor Lane missed the cut for the National and was well-beaten in a lesser race over the Aintree fences.

It doesn't always pay us to take a view, even when we get it right.

Back in 1992, we came to the conclusion that Carvill's Hill was very beatable in the Cheltenham Gold Cup. He'd put up all his best performances on reasonably flat tracks on soft ground, but the big race would be run round an undulating course on ground that was likely to be good.

He was very popular with punters and we saw a lot of money for him but we held the price and were vindicated when he could finish only fifth, over 60 lengths behind the 25-1 winner Cool Ground. It looked like being a really good result for us and there was a certain amount of euphoria immediately afterwards, but we soon learned of a serious downside.

A punter called Dick Mussell had placed a £7 five-leg accumulator in one of our shops. All his picks won – and Cool Ground was the last leg! For that one bet, we had to pay out £600,000. I'm sure we won't get much sympathy, but wins like that wipe out a lot of losing fivers and tenners on the favourite!

---

**JEREMY SCOTT**
*Tote*

THERE is little to top the high-risk, high-return strategy of betting ante-post when it comes to maximising the drama, suspense and value involved in having a bet – and that's just for the punters!

For the odds-compilers at the Tote, pricing up races ante-post is a way to generate interest in and turnover on a race at an early stage. However, with liabilities able to spiral in minutes and a wrong price costing the firm millions, the drama can quickly turn into a crisis!

Getting the price right is, therefore, essential. To do it, you need to combine an extensive knowledge of racing with a good grasp of mathematics, sound personal convictions and just a pinch of luck.

Trends in yards are the essential starting point when setting the framework for the ante-post book. Horses from shrewd top yards are always the ones to be wary of and reputation alone often ensures they will never be far from the top of the market.

Any punter worth their salt will appreciate the importance of the going in determining a horse's chances in a particular race, which, along with the distance, would be the next two key variables the odds-compilers would account for.

Obviously, with ante-post markets the going cannot be determined months in advance and here research into previous trends at the meetings will be taken into consideration. Pedigrees will be analysed alongside recent form to give an indication of how suited each horse is to the trip.

Once all the available knowledge and information has been applied, the book is complete, other than attributing the 'x' factor to the runners. This requires a very personal touch from the odds-compiler, in which they account for the popularity of a horse and the likelihood of a public gamble.

Being able to gauge this is essential. Some horses just capture the public's imagination and, although they may not look a threat in the race, they can quickly become a big threat in the book.

People often forget that what a bookmaker does is 'make a book' and not just lay horses. For, despite all the tireless work that goes into making an ante-post market, there comes a point where it becomes a matter of mathematical juggling and sheer volume of money will force prices down and affect the whole market.

**VICTOR CHANDLER**
*Victor Chandler International*

JUST as horseracing and betting on it has undergone a big change in recent years, my own life is vastly different now from what it was just a few short years ago.

When I decided to take the bulk of my business to Gibraltar, it was with the idea of giving new life to betting, which, at the time, was being strangled by the nine per cent off-course deduction to punters.

Cynics said that getting rid of the deduction would be to the detriment of the revenues to the sport. The 2002 Grand National will have finally blown away all those misguided opinions.

First estimates were of an 80 per cent increase in betting levels on a year earlier. Not only is betting more easily transacted, but it has become more inclusive; there is a much greater likelihood of women feeling comfortable in a betting shop environment, such has been the change in opinions and the attractiveness of the shops themselves in a short time.

It's a nice feeling to be credited with being an influence in the change. I'm sure that, without someone breaking ranks and being more competitive initially than the major opposition, there would not have been any hope of a catalyst to pave the way to the present status quo. Now, everyone says (including, most importantly, the government) that it makes more sense to base funding of racing on bookmakers' profits, rather than a system linked to turnover.

At the same time, predictions that Victor Chandler might now return en bloc from Gibraltar to England, with the arrival of tax-free betting there, were also wide of the mark. We have a core domestic racecourse organisation which operates very comfortably, but the highly-trained multi-lingual staff in our Gibraltar headquarters is ideal for the requirements of our many Far East clients.

Football betting has become very important to us and to all bookmaking firms, and the 2002 World Cup will, as I write, shortly be the focus of another major increase.

My own real love is to revert to my natural instincts at the big race meetings, like

Cheltenham or Royal Ascot. Like J P McManus and Michael Tabor, I am, at heart, a punter and even when the firm's experts have a particular slant on a race, I often have my own opinion.

The biggest wins (and, by definition, losses) have been as a result of taking that opinion to its extreme and either laying short-priced favourites, at Cheltenham especially, to large sums, or unearthing long-priced horses which could upset them.

If I have a simple rule, it is not to back short-priced horses. There are so many things that can go wrong in the case of a hot favourite. Obvious factors, like unfavourable going or, on the Flat, a bad draw, might seem fundamental to the student of the game, but can be major pitfalls for the uninitiated.

Many people cite the concept of value in order to draw a theoretical line above which one would have a bet and below which one would abstain. I think that is simplistic, especially as, nowadays, we are seeing an element of trade collusion in terms of increasingly over-round books.

Previously, prices were artificially contracted by the activity of the Big Four firms, shortening horses that were obvious liabilities in the shops. Now, such action is almost futile, but has been rendered unnecessary anyway because course bookmakers have become realists.

When their pitches were first deregulated and opened up for sale, newcomers from other aspects of business life thought this a way to mint money. The harsh reality for many of them, keen to offer unwise bigger odds on 'live' horses, has been a short shelf-life for people who did not know the game.

Some long-serving members of the on-course betting rings, and I think they deserved it, got out with a nice few bob to help their retirement. Those who remain can look forward to a reasonable return in most instances, especially as the daily exposure to races in so many more homes will increase familiarity with the sport, and the wish to attend the races.

I'll close with this thought about value. For me, it's a gut feeling; if a horse should be 10-1 and it's 25s, I'll go for it in a big way. I suppose the slogan I would attach to that element of my betting, and therefore my advice in these pages, is 'never be afraid to win too much.'

**SIMON CLARE**
*Coral*

ODDS-COMPILATION is an art, not a science and don't let anyone convince you otherwise. All those maths lessons spent learning about percentages, ratios and the like may come in handy but, when it comes to issuing prices about horses, the best odds compilers in the business use a healthy slice of instinct and gut feel.

The list of facts and variables that have to be taken into account when assessing each horse's chance of victory is almost limitless; countless books on the subject have been published and are now serving very useful careers as doorstops. They are, of course, well worth reading but it is the individual interpretation that sorts the men from the boys. I am by no means an expert odds-compiler, indeed the Coral trading team are probably planning a low-grade juvenile novice campaign for me as we speak, but I do throw my hat into the ring on occasions, particularly when it comes to ante-post betting.

Pricing up ante-post races is a more forgiving medium than compiling odds at the overnight declaration stage. The stakes are far higher for the latter, as these prices will be published alongside all the competitors' odds, while numerous newspaper tipsters, most notably Pricewise in the Racing Post, will be circling like vultures, seeking to expose any perceived generosity.

With ante-post betting, bookmakers are afforded the extra reprieve of a horse not making the race through injury or change of plan. A recent example of how 'lady luck' can assist a bookmaker, even when he has offered an over-generous price, occurred when the 2001 Cheltenham Festival was abandoned.

Three years before, a Coral telephone betting customer asked me for odds on Istabraq winning three more Champion hurdles following his first scintillating success. I did a quick calculation in my head, a head slightly blurred by a glass or two of fine white wine, and quoted 66-1. The customer maintained his poker face, placed £500 at the price and walked off smiling like the proverbial Cheshire Cat.

The true odds should probably have been 40-1, as I was reminded on many subsequent occasions. When Istabraq was 1-3 to complete a historic fourth Champion Hurdle victory, the customer concerned could have been forgiven for planning how to spend his money.

What could never have been foreseen was the awful arrival of the Foot And Mouth epidemic that blighted the farming industry and caused the racing industry to slow down to a standstill. The Festival was called off and, while Istabraq started second-favourite for the race a year later, the bet went down when he pulled up after just two flights.

How many times have you backed a horse ante-post at massive odds, felt smug as the odds tumbled to single figures in the lead up to the race, only to see the horse beaten out of sight. Yet any ante-post punter will tell you that the gain is definitely worth all the pain.

In my first week representing Coral many years ago, I headed off to The Curragh for the Irish 2,000 Guineas expecting a fairly easy day in the sunshine. A nicely-bred juvenile colt trained by Aidan O'Brien won a six-furlong maiden at 1-3 and a few of the English racing journalists asked me for a price for the following year's 2,000 Guineas, nearly twelve months later.

I offered what I considered rather stingy odds of 25-1, only to find a queue of racing hacks trying to bite my hands off for a bet at those odds. The horse's name was King Of Kings and the rest is history. I am still here to tell the tale, albeit as quietly and rarely as possible.

# CHAPTER 4
# READING THE MARKET

 LAYING the odds has proved a ruinous pursuit for those who wager indiscriminately. Today, with too many on-course bookmakers chasing after too little money, the pendulum has swung in favour of the on-course professional.

In many instances, until the blower moves in, prices can increase to the benefit of those who can tell at a glance when 1-2 really represents 1-7. In reverse, they can pinpoint the occasion when 8-13 should read 5-4, placing them in an advantageous position (the only place to be with so much against you).

Off-course, backing anything on a regular basis under 2-1 is an expensive luxury. Genuine odds-on chances must only be used as 'lifelines', or as bankers for pool bets like the Jackpot or the Placepot.

False favourites must be taken advantage of; if you can define them, this will place you several lengths clear of the average punter and their shortcomings will boost your dividends at the expense of their stakes.

Don't be tempted into doubling or trebling short-priced horses on a daily basis, unless you want to ingratiate yourself with the betting shop manager. On rare occasions, it is acceptable to couple a pair of good things, but don't make a habit out of it – see Chapter 11 of this book for more advice about betting at short prices.

In betting, time is on your side. Bookmakers are in business to take money and offer prices, but it is up to you to desist until you are confident of success.

In order to obtain a 'fair' price, hopefully above the SP, there are a few things to take into account.

The 'first show' is the first price list relayed to the betting shop. Generally, you can afford to wait; the cream of the Tattersalls odds has already been skimmed by astute punters and rails clerks.

Prices tend to drift back when the rails betting opens (reflected in the second and third shows), but don't wait for too long, for, unless you are looking at a genuine drifter, blower money will shorten up the leading fancies, with the SP being of prime importance for the betting shop.

A typical show for a favourite today might be:

11-10, 5-4, 11-8, 6-5, returned at 11-10.

So don't complain if you back a winner at SP – on occasion, you must expect to 'pay the fine'.

It is only through experience gained over many years on a racecourse that the pro can interpret the machinations of the market. Sense and sensitivity prevail. Pros can distinguish between horses shortening through genuine professional and public support and those tightening up via the blower.

Stable or professional money would see radical price cuts from the moment the phones start ringing, even before the opening of the betting shop doors. Subsequently, the on-course market sees easing, as on-track layers with no previous liabilities try to make their books – if it's a true coup, you can be sure the blower will trim the odds again for the SP.

Early morning prices can offer good value – the leading bookies look on this as a little window-dressing akin to free advertising, but they don't expect to make much from the exercise. Their protection is to exercise their option on how much they are prepared to lay, which usually keeps their risk to a minimum at all but the top meetings.

It is the smaller player who can benefit here. Large punters, unless professional losers, can never expect to be accommodated in full.

Phone lines and tipping services with subscribers can have a marked effect on the morning price fluctuations, with many moderate-to-heavy players all wanting to back the same horse. On occasions, this 'hot' money can make your market. You can profit accordingly, but must note all serious early moves.

Unfair as it may seem, the credit punter has the advantage over his cash counterpart by an hour, as the phone lines open before the shops. This helps the bookmaker, as he gets a 'lead' to the informed move before opening time.

Don't accept a dried-up price mid-morning. If it does fail to drift back during the SIS shows, grit your teeth and let it run. It might win, but the value is lost.

With morning prices offered daily, all-in run or not, advance betting has lost much of its attraction. Don't get carried away when the press give rave notices to an animal which slaughters its maiden opposition – it must prove itself in Group company before being considered for a Classic.

You might lose out on a price but it is generally better to wait until you can bet at 'non-runner, no bet'. Twenty years ago, apart from the five Classics, the spring and autumn doubles and a few big handicaps, punters had to wait for the course market to be formed before taking a price. Nowadays, you can afford to be choosy. The road to the punter's graveyard is paved with vouchers destined for Ante's inferno.

Though a mind like a pocket calculator can be an invaluable asset in this game, only a few basic features of it are required to see, at a glance, how bad the figures are on the opening show and that most must lengthen or be exposed to ridicule.

The mid-market usually sees the lowest percentage over-round, so that odds are then most in favour of the backer. Greyhound racing, most Irish turf meetings, races with big fields and 'National Hunt' flat races most commonly see percentages stacked in favour of the 'house'.

With so much information on offer, betting shop screens should also carry the overall percentage, fluctuating as the market develops. This would enable backers to assess the situation and see when bargains are thin on the ground.

The market revolves around opinion and argument, with prices fluctuating through demand or lack of it.

We're often told 'There's a gamble taking place' but, at a conservative estimate, possibly only one in ten of the gambles we hear about actually deserves the name, when sheer weight of money forces the price down – a real gamble snowballing from an inspired source, with the public joining in.

'Shortening in price' would be a safer and more accurate phrase to use on most occasions.

Certain stables rarely win with drifting debutants or lightly-raced horses, whilst others can upset calculations, defying apparent lack of support to skate up. Those familiar with riding arrangements for leading stables are in a position to assess in advance whether the stable are expecting a winner.

There are numerous reasons why horses can shorten up and others drift.

The most obvious reason for a horse shortening in price is that it has been tipped by 'Pricewise' in the *Racing Post*, now the country's most influential tipster. I'm sure we've all had the experience of opening the *Post* on a Saturday and groaning, because 'Pricewise' has tipped the horse that we fancied and its price will therefore be shorter than it would have been.

Some telephone tipping lines can have a similar effect on a horse's price.

A leading rider on a roll at a major meeting will often be the subject of accumulators in the betting shops, in which case money from the shops will be sent to the course to force down the SPs on his later mounts, if the earlier ones win.

A classic example of this occurred in September 1996, when Frankie Dettori rode all seven winners at Ascot. His last ride, Fujiyama Crest, was running in a very competitive 18-runner handicap and had been forecast in the morning papers to start at double-figure odds.

However, Frankie had won the first six races. Punters around the country had put accumulators on him that morning, as happened every Saturday, and, although the stakes were generally small, the payout after six wins was already going to be huge and would be catastrophic for the bookies if the seventh horse won.

So the leading firms sent thousands of pounds to Ascot to compress the SP of Fujiyama Crest, with the result that it went off at 2-1. All semblance of value had long gone, but the horse won, nonetheless, albeit only by a neck, to complete the layers' nightmare. A horse might also shorten in price simply through lack of support for its market rivals. I've certainly seen the outsider of five shorten for no reason other than the first four in the betting were all 'on the drift'.

In that case, there was no gamble on the outsider, though it was possibly nibbled at by one or two shrewd punters, including those bookmakers not averse to a bet on an outsider when unable to 'get' the favourite.

Often, horses with paper form, popular with the press and in the shops but not attracting much money on the course, will initially slide and then shorten in price as the off-course money is 'blown' to the track.

Even though no concerted gamble has occurred, this is legitimate business – the off-course bookies are balancing their books according to demand or lack of it.

Many times, an outsider has moved from, say, 20-1 all the way into 14-1 with no recorded bet of any significance – another example of value-seekers fielding against market leaders that are considered to be poor value.

Interpreting the market is complex in the extreme, a highly-specialised field with decades of experience a prerequisite. Gone are the days of simplicity when fancied horses shortened in price and those not fancied went out.

When betting in 2002, regard betting as 99.9% straight, even though the next show of prices may be hard to predict. Money still talks, but on too many occasions, it talks with a forked tongue.

---

A successful bookmaker with pitches around the south of England, **BARRY DENNIS** has a no-nonsense style that's made him television's favourite bookie. Appearing regularly on Channel 4 and Attheraces, he's best known for nominating his 'Bismarcks' (fancied horses that he reckons are bad value for punters).

## You Too Can Be a Racecourse Pro, With Practice

WHAT punters can learn on the track depends on whether they're on a social day out or are regular racegoers with a view to serious betting. They should always visit the parade ring and become adept at noticing fit horses. This is only learnt by experience but a good tip is that the horse must look lean, alert and their eyes must be taking in everything that's around them.

Even more important is to watch the horses going to post, especially younger horses, aged two and three. You must always take note of horses that appear to be enjoying the experience of going to post.

As for racecourse rumour, it can't hurt for punters to get to know the professional gamblers that always loiter near rails bookmakers (Dave Nevison is one of them, though I wouldn't recommend that anyone try copying what he does!). Then, when those guys make a move, the punters must try to be one step ahead of them, or at least right next to them, backing the horses they're trying to back.

If you're experienced enough to follow the right market moves, it's a big benefit.

Obviously, even I can't be right every time but generally, through fifty years of experience, I've learned to separate good information from bad, which is something only experience and practice can give. For example, although trainers use runners to put their money on, we get to know who the runners are, so their presence is a tip in itself.

To become an experienced on-course gambler/punter, you'd need to attend racecourses on a very regular basis – probably at least two hundred times a year.

---

*Now 40, **ANDY SMITH** has been involved in racecourse bookmaking since he was at school, when his father had a pitch at Newton Abbot and he was often taken along to lend a hand.*
*Based in the south-west, he has spent over half a million pounds in recent years, acquiring pitches at racecourses around the country, including two at Cheltenham.*

## Serious Punters Must Come Racing

AS a racecourse bookie, you won't be surprised to hear that I think punters get a much better deal by coming racing than they would by spending all day in a betting shop. But there's a very good reason for this – if you're looking for a bit of value, trying to find the best price available about a particular horse, you can get a real edge at the track.

Only the other day, I was laying a favourite at 2-1 and that was still the price on my board at the 'off' but the horse, who got beat, was returned at 13-8. Just by shopping around in the on-course market, you can almost always do better than the returned price. SP returns are not what they should be.

Anyone stuck in a bookies can either bet at SP or on the prices put up by SIS, which don't always include the best price available at the track. Last week, a horse opened at 5-1 on the shop screens after being laid to take thousands out of the ring at 6-1. Of course, the lion's share of SIS is owned by the big bookies, so you could argue that there's a very obvious reason for that sort of thing happening.

If you believe, as I do, that value betting is the only way to win money in the long term, then you've got a much better chance of getting a value price from the on-course market.

When I'm going racing, I'll price up every race in advance, either getting up very early in the morning or starting work the night before. When I'm setting prices, I'm weighing up each horse's winning chance, rather than how I expect the market to be. I'm looking to bet to around 112% or 114%. Quite often, you see *Racing Post* forecasts set to much larger margins, so the prices I offer will generally be bigger. I look for horses with form on the going or form at the track, or horses from yards that are currently doing well.

With so much racing on these days, it's hard to keep an eye on everything that's happening, so I specialise in jumps racing in the south.

As well as being a bookmaker, I enjoy having a punt myself and I'll back a horse when I think its price offers value, i.e. when it's on offer at a bigger price than I make it. I think each-way offers tremendous value for punters. I've just been looking at an eighteen-runner handicap in which ten wouldn't hit the frame if they started this morning, so in that race you can effectively get a quarter the odds each-way for four places in an eight-runner race.

Equally, I'll lay a horse at a bigger price than is generally available, if I've taken a view that the current price exaggerates its chance.

I'm aware of the recent developments with internet betting exchanges and I've been keeping an eye on them. I can see that they sometimes offer great value if you're a punter but you've always got to ask yourself if you could be betting against someone who knows a bit more than you.

The problem with betting exchanges is that they're so open to corruption. They've made it easy to lay one horse in a race, so in theory it's possible for connections to lay their own horse, anonymously, if they know for some reason that it's not going to win.

Punters aren't the mugs they used to be. With the *Racing Post*, the internet and tipping phone lines, they're more clued up than ever before. Even so, they still have some bad habits.

The worst, of course, is that they chase their losses.

I always think there's never a last race. You should always remember that there are going to be another nine thousand races in the year after the one you've lost on, so you should treat every race as though it's the first of the day and have as much on as if there was the whole day's racing still to go.

An instantly recognisable figure at Southern tracks, **GARY WILTSHIRE** has been a racecourse bookmaker for 20 years and is also to be seen as an occasional pundit on Attheraces and the Racing Channel. He has recently launched his own person-to-person betting exchange on the web at www.garywiltshire.com.

## These Are Great Days for On-course Shrewdies

THE biggest advantage for those at the track is that you get to see what the horses look like before placing a bet. Even though I have to spend most of my time in the ring, I always go round to the paddock to have a look at them before every race.

I'm looking for negative signs, mostly; if a horse is sweating up or if it looks unfit, you know that its winning chance is much less than most punters would think from just reading the form.

At the track, you also get to follow the market in a much more meaningful way than you can from the betting shops, where only some of the price changes are flagged up. There are basically two reasons for a horse shortening in price – either there's been proper on-course money for it, or else Ladbrokes or Hills have been backing it, to reduce its SP and recover some of their liabilities.

Watching from a betting shop, you can't tell the difference between these two possibilities. But if you're there in the ring, you can see whether the money's coming from professional gamblers (whose judgement merits respect) or from the off-course firms, in which case it's just a reflection of what punters generally have been backing.

People following the smart money round the courses really do have a chance. I'd say there are more shrewd people going racing now than I've ever known and, coming up to the 2002 Flat season, the on-course bookies have had their worst ever year. There are so many publications available to punters now, as well as computer banks and so on, there's never been a time when they've been better-informed.

When I'm pricing up a day's racing, I always start with the *Racing Post* – the same information that's available to any gambler and which is stuck to the walls of betting shops all round the country.

Also, online betting exchanges are a really important development – they're the way forward, for my money. If they don't like the look of a fancied runner, punters can play bookmaker and lay it, instead of having to find one to beat it.

Bookmakers do use these exchanges from the racecourse to balance the books. I've just opened my own and I'm very hopeful it'll be a success.

Generally, punters will get their best value from win singles and each-way bets. If you stick to those kinds of bets, you won't go far wrong. I think each-way betting really tips the balance in favour of punters, especially when it pays down to fourth place, which is why I only accept win bets at the track.

The Placepot also offers tremendous value for punters. For a small stake, you can win plenty, especially at the smaller meetings, and you don't have to find the winners.

Combination bets, doubles, trebles and so on, should be avoided if you're a punter, because they favour the bookies. Saying that, it can pay really well if it goes right – I was one of many that suffered when Frankie Dettori rode all seven winners at Ascot. In just over an hour, I lost £500,000.

# CHAPTER 5
# CHOOSING HOW TO BET

*NICK FOX was a Naps table and dual Press Challenge winner as 'Templegate' of The Sun. Since joining the Racing Post in 1999, his daily advised bets in Betting Bureau have shown a healthy profit. He looks for high value, usually at big prices, and says punters face a choice; back the horses everyone else wants to back and enjoy a high strike-rate (winners to bets ratio) of winners but an inevitable long-term loss, or oppose the crowd, accept a low strike-rate and give yourself the chance of decent long-term profits. 'My strike-rate for the early-price races during the last jumps season was an embarrassing 16% (six winners from 38 bets) but these bets yielded a profit of more than 47%,' he says.*

AS far as getting a bet on is concerned, there's never been a better time to be a punter. In addition to the bookmakers and the Tote, which have been around for ages, there's now the opportunity to make the most of recent innovations, like spread betting and internet betting exchanges.

Each of these four betting outlets offers advantages and disadvantages. Here's my form guide to each.

## Bookmakers

THESE guys must be getting worried. They had the racing market virtually to themselves for decades and now face strong, fast-growing competition. A few years ago, there were two tough tasks facing those seeking to bet profitably. The first was finding the right horse at the right price, the second was getting the bet on for a worthwhile amount. On top of both, there was the dreaded off-course betting tax.

Bookmakers should really be separated into two categories. First, there's the big high street chains, who don't like to take any risk at all and who, when they're out of line with the competition in offering early prices, are very quick to stop punters taking advantage. Second, there's the on-course bookies, many of whom do take risks and are willing to back their view with their own cash.

### Pros

*1) Familiarity – this is the form of betting we all grew up with.*

*2) Punters know their full liability in advance of the race, as well as the amount they stand to win.*

*3) The abolition of betting tax has made betting shops far more competitive.*

*4) The shops are a good place for multiple bets, doubles, trebles etc.*

*5) The chains do make mistakes with their early offers – if you can get on. There's also the sociability of being in the betting shop.*

### Cons

*1) This type of betting is looking dated and suffers from being one-dimensional: you back a horse to win or win and place and that's about all. There's no opportunity to bet against a horse winning, as with spread firms and betting exchanges. To do so, a punter would have to back every other horse in the race.*

*2) It's often hard to get on the steamers to any worthwhile amount.*

*3) Numbers games are a serious turn-off.*

## The Tote

TO understand when it might be best to bet on the Tote, it's important to know how it works.

All bets for a race are pooled and the Tote – mistakenly, in my view – takes out a set amount of 16% from the win pool and (an exorbitant) 24% from the place pool. The problem with this is that on-course bookmakers can be betting to a margin of only around 5% on small-field races, so in such cases it's hardly worth the effort to look at the Tote boards.

Where the Tote scores is in big-field handicaps, when the bookmakers are betting to far bigger margins, sometimes well over 40%. Then, the Tote starts to look attractive. It's also well-known that Tote punters have a tendency to overbet horses from big yards with well-known jockeys, like Pat Eddery.

If you want two examples of when the Tote is likely to fare very badly or very well against the book, then these are mine:

**Bad Tote Bet:** *A fancied horse trained by John Dunlop and ridden by Pat Eddery in a five-runner non-handicap.*

**Good Tote Bet:** *A 20-1 or bigger chance, trained by An Unknown and ridden by A Claimer in a 30-runner handicap.*

**Pros**

1) You can get very big dividends on the horses the betting public isn't mad about.
2) There can be huge value when dead money builds up in bets like the Scoop6.
3) In most cases, there are no limits on the amount you can bet.
4) Watch out for late gambles on the book which the Tote punters often fail to notice. Consider an exacta with the field for such horses.

**Cons**

1) You don't know what odds you will get until after the race and you can't take a price.
2) The markets can be dreadfully weak and even a small bet in a place pool at some tracks can affect the dividend significantly.
3) A set take-out irrespective of the number of runners usually makes Tote betting a no-go in small-field races.
4) The place take-out is too big.

# Spread Betting

THE spread firms are no longer the new kids on the block and have rightly built up a big business by offering a more sophisticated form of betting, in which it is possible to back against horses doing well.

If you believe a horse will run poorly for whatever reason, you often have the opportunity to sell its finishing position, or sell it on a length-by-length basis against a horse who you fancy to run well. The advantage of this type of betting is that you don't even need to find the winner and there are opportunities to bet even when you haven't got a clue which of several horses might win the race. The golden rule for spread betting is: always consider the worst case scenario and bet to a stake that allows for when this happens.

**Pros**

1) There are more opportunities for good value betting, even when you're not confident of finding the winner.
2) You can bet on a horse running badly.
3) The more right you are, the more you win.

## Cons

1) Spread betting can be hard for newcomers to grasp and it's certainly not for those who don't fully understand how it works.

2) The more wrong you are the more you lose.

3) Those who don't bet to the golden rule (above) can lose far more than they anticipated.

## Internet Betting Exchanges

NOW you can play bookmaker and lay your own prices against horses you don't think will win, or even try to lay all the field in a race and make your own book.

Betting exchanges, led by the likes of Betfair and Betdaq, are the fastest-growing betting businesses around. Again, you don't need to find the winner. Correctly anticipate which horse might be backed and you can bet on it at, say, 8-1 and (if all works well) lay it back before the race at, say, 6-1. Then, you've got a guaranteed profit whether the horse wins or falls at the first.

### Pros

1) The prices offered are usually better than those offered by bookmakers.

2) You have the opportunity to bet against a horse winning.

3) There's the chance to take your profit, even before the race has started.

4) It's easy to place bets and you get quick settlement.

### Cons

1) Commission has to be paid to the site operator.

2) Debit and credit card betting can cause problems if you're prone to gambling, rather than sensible betting.

## Conclusions

WHICHEVER way you bet currently, it would be wrong not to consider all the opportunities available.

The bookmaker may be best in one case, the spread firm in another. But if you take your betting seriously, you should feel pleased that there has never been a better time for we backers, although the old problem remains: in the end, you still have to find the right horse at the right price.

# CHAPTER 6
# AT THE TRACK

**SIMON HOLT** took over from Graeme Goode as Channel 4's main commentator at the beginning of 2000 and is now firmly established as 'the voice of racing.' He writes a weekly column for Raceform On Saturday.

## Find the Winners and Keep Your Figure

FOR me, there is no better way to spend an afternoon than at the races and, aside from the healthy and exciting outdoor sporting atmosphere, it is also still the best place to have a bet.

Nowadays, there are so many betting options for punters, whether it be betting shops, telephone accounts or, increasingly, via the internet. But it is still difficult to beat being paid out in warm readies at the racecourse where, with a bit of shopping around, you might also 'burgle' a point or two above SP.

I know of at least one professional punter who turned against the track last year in favour of placing his bets on a home computer but, within six months, he found his new life so soulless that he was soon back on the road. On his return, he looked rather pale (too much time spent indoors) and there was much more of him than before, his waistline having swollen dramatically as a result of regular 'tea-and-biscuit' breaks.

Apart from missing his racing buddies, my fatter friend also found that one important element to his betting was missing: the chance to check out the appearance of the horses in the paddock.

In these days of wall-to-wall television coverage of racing, this is probably the single most significant advantage of actually visiting the racecourse, as, with a keen eye and a bit of experience, much money can be won – and saved – by observing the horses' health and wellbeing.

To become a 'judge', you don't necessarily need to know the difference between a pastern and a fetlock. Paddock-watching is a fairly inexact science, given that horses come in all shapes and sizes – they most certainly do not 'all look the same' as my father has always maintained – and, although there are a few general rules of thumb, one will develop personal preferences.

Judging a horse's fitness is common sense. Has the horse got a big tummy? What about signs of muscle definition on the neck and hind quarters? Does his coat glow with health or is it dull and cold?

The last point can sometimes be misleading, depending on the time of year and whether the horse is a full horse (a colt) or a gelding (whose coats tend to shine less).

A personal priority is the horse's demeanour and body language. I like to see a horse walking purposefully (but not over-excitedly) and showing plenty of interest in his surroundings. There is a fine line here; a horse who carts his lad round the parade ring is probably running his race before it starts, whereas one that lollops round is hardly giving the impression of being 'up' for the task ahead. In contrast, sweating is not a particularly good sign (especially behind the saddle and on a cold day), but its true significance depends on whether the horse is known to be a free sweater or not.

Sizing up unraced horses is always interesting and, in particular, I love to visit the parade ring before two-year-old races. Watch out for good walkers – horses who stretch and point their toe – and those animals that look proportioned. Many young horses are unfurnished; their back end may be higher than the front and they may also be green, so take note if they are skittish, colty or noisy.

In horses that have had a lot of racing, check that they do not look too hard-trained, 'tucked up' and light beforehand and if their coat is not too dull. These may be signs that they have had enough for the time being.

Personally, I always look for horses with scope, especially in a race of inexperienced horses. But the scopey type, while maybe one for the future, may not necessarily be the one for today. One other thing: I dislike horses who carry their heads too high, even at the walk. In my view, it's usually a sign of poor temperament and an undesirable racing attitude.

From the parade ring, it is often a good idea to make a bolt for the stands as soon as the jockeys are in the saddle, so as to watch the horses move to post. I find this particularly useful in Flat races (jumpers often go very steadily to the start), and especially when the ground is quite firm.

Horses who stretch, and skim the surface on fast ground are definitely worth considering for a bet, whereas few animals who either show a markedly round action or 'scratch' to post will show their best form on an unforgiving surface. The latter types tend (a generalisation) to prefer softer conditions.

These clues are most significant in young, unproven horses, where the form book offers little or no guide to their preferences.

To conclude, here's one more nugget of advice. The racecourse is a wonderful place. It's friendly, exciting and spectacular. It's also a place where there is more gossip and rumours circulating than at ten ladies' coffee mornings.

Punters never seem to learn. If I had a pound for every time I've been asked 'got any tips?' in the last 15 years, my wealth might be quite enviable.

Take it from me: most tips are trash and racecourse rumours are usually rubbish. Have faith in your own instincts and your own observations and you will back more winners, and enjoy them more.

Had I practised this preaching over the years, it would be smooth Havanas and not these cheap and disgusting panatellas which have been staining my office walls during the writing of this article.

---

**GERALD DELAMERE** *is a highly respected judge of racehorses. He began writing for the* Weekender *in 1989 and his column is essential reading for form students. Delamere has also been a successful tipster for the* Sporting Life *and the* Racing Post, *flagging up Best Mate as a future Gold Cup winner after the horse's very first run, in a bumper two and a half years before his Cheltenham triumph.*

## An Expert's Guide to Paddock-watching

WHILE form and stats are facts and in the formbook, a view from the paddock is very much in the eye of the beholder. This area is quite abstract because a horse can often look very different in the pre-parade compared to the main paddock, and yet again when mounted.

It is far from being an exact science. Over 20 years ago, my paddock interpretation mainly centred on how a horse looked in its coat and whether it sweated up or not. I was on course the day Arkle made his racecourse debut at my local track, Mullingar in December 1961; sadly, the significance of the great event didn't strike a chord until much later.

Having viewed chasers all winter, it's a real culture shock come Easter, with juveniles at Kempton. Fitness is paramount at this stage and there are two main areas to look at. A definition of the horse's ribs confirms fitness, while slackness in front or behind doesn't.

The amount of work a horse has done is also displayed by how well the muscle lines have developed down his hind quarters. A sprinter in midsummer should be a ball of muscle.

The round-barrelled gelding is the one that can catch you out – it often appears to be carrying condition, whereas this is simply the make and shape of the animal. Make a note of such types and don't get caught a second time.

The classy two-mile chaser Tiutchev is a case in point. He always looks too big on his reappearance and even sometimes on his second outing.

The size and shape of a colt or filly is a vast area for discussion and will only be touched on here. I don't go into how correct a horse is, as a bloodstock agent would before the sales, otherwise you would never back a horse after paddock inspection.

I prefer a strongly-made animal with size and scope and will always be wary of the small, narrow type when they are asked to carry a big weight.

The area near the girth from the withers downwards needs plenty of depth for heartroom. A horse's neck has to be in proportion to its body. One that goes straight up with just a short neck is not attractive.

A long back can lead to weakness and then unsoundness. You like to see a horse's hindquarters well rounded – it shouldn't have cow hips or be angular, while its hocks shouldn't be too wide or too close together.

The head is most important – it can tell so much about the character of an animal and its potential willingness to race. I don't like piggy little ears, parrot-mouths or too much white about the eye.

Alertness is necessary when walking around and a horse with its head down can denote a lack of interest or enthusiasm. Many insist that a horse should walk well and use himself properly, as it suggests that, when he gallops, he won't be knocking into itself. The subject of sweating is a major paddock factor and one of the most difficult to have hard and fast opinions about. In February 2002, Jimmy Tennis made his British debut at Ascot and came into the paddock with sweat dripping off his belly. No-one knew if that was normal for the ex-French gelding and it would have put many off, but he won just the same.

The normal perception of sweating is that there is anxiety in the horse's mind concerning what he or she is about to be asked to do. It is important to know the regular sweaters and those whose performances aren't affected by it.

When sweating takes the form of a foamy secretion between the hind legs, which I call the 'shaving brush', it doesn't worry me as much as most watchers, but frothing at the mouth can be a worrying sign. Sweating in front of the saddle is less worrying than behind or under the saddlecloth.

What about jig-jogging, or when a horse is on his or her toes? Neither bothers me too much, unless the animal is fractious, edgy or sweating as well.

A horse that is pulling the lad or girl around the ring, full of vitality, was aptly described once by a well-known Irish breeder as being 'mad for the road' – a positive sign. However, you can often see a horse float around the paddock with well-being and that is the type that I like.

**ALAN AMIES** *joined Raceform on leaving school and worked for them for 35 years, becoming the country's most respected race-reader. In retirement, there's no danger of him losing interest in the game; indeed, he enjoys regular betting trips to Hong Kong.*

## There's Plenty to Learn if You're Paying Attention

PUNTERS on the course have a definite advantage over those in the betting shop, principally because it's so important to have a look at the horses before you have a bet. With two-year-olds, it's absolutely essential to have a look at them before risking your money.

What you have to look for is something you can only learn with experience, it's a question of learning by trial and error. I never had any training for it, but I learned just by spending time at the track, talking with other regulars and swapping views.

Eventually, when you see the right horse, looking fit and well, it really hits you smack in the face.

I'm always especially concerned to look for horses that might be getting a bit edgy, boiling over or going too freely to post. Even when you can't see a horse that looks particularly well, you can often rule out a few and that's important, as you can save yourself what would have been a losing bet.

As well as looking at them in the paddock, you should also take note of how the runners go down to the start and the way they move, which can often persuade you whether to have a bet or not. In the winter, this becomes still more important, as the horses' rugs aren't taken off until they get onto the course, so this is your first chance to judge their physique.

Although sprinters are generally poor movers, so you can't take too much note of that, you'd certainly want to see a stayer moving well to post.

Jumpers frequently go slowly to post, which means you can't tell a thing, and you have to pay attention to the surface – when horses are going downhill towards the start, as they do at Beverley, they can't be blamed for not stretching out.

If you take your betting seriously and have a proper look at the horses, you'll quite often find that you miss the best price in the betting ring. That's unfortunate, but the priority has to be a thorough assessment of the runners and, as long as you can be sure that you're happy with your choice, there's less reason to worry about the odds you're taking.

If you can't make it to the track, you can usually get some sort of look at the horses if the race is on television, though I go bananas when they don't show the horses until near the start.

Assessing the horses before the race is impossible from a bookie's shop, where the screens typically cut to the race just in time for the 'off'.

There's a lot to see and hear at the track but you have to be careful about how you use anything you learn when you're betting. I haven't found racecourse rumour to be at all helpful or reliable, though, of course, it depends on the source – you get to learn who's a reliable judge and who isn't.

Sometimes, when you see that a trainer's come to the races to saddle a runner, then you know that's significant because it's a trainer you don't generally see at the track; perhaps he's very busy, or doesn't like to travel far. On the other hand, his presence might be explained by the fact that he's got a difficult owner and he's come along to try and keep that owner happy.

You hear stories about trainers who've been spotted in the ring, backing one of their runners, but I'm not sure if that should make *you* think about backing the horse as well. I usually think that, if the trainer were capable of organising a serious coup, he'd get other people to place the bets for him.

If you're a regular at a particular course, you'll find it gets easier to weigh up the state of the going and the effect that'll have on the way races are run. I've always found that a course responds differently to watering than it does to sudden rain – for example, in sprint races at Thirsk, they can win from either extreme of the draw if the ground's bad, but if the track's been watered, the stands-side runners have a real edge.

The other real advantage that you have at the track is benefiting from the on-course market, which gives you much more choice than if you were just stood in one firm's shop. At some tracks, the market is so strong that there's almost no automatic profit for the bookies.

That's especially true in Scotland, where it seems the bookies are generally more prepared to take a bet.

I've found some very good-priced winners just from being at the races, but I'd very much doubt if you could make a long-term profit from a betting shop, even in these times of zero deductions.

**RICHARD AUSTEN** *is a racing journalist. He worked at Timeform for ten years before turning freelance in 1997.*

## Whatever Your Betting Foibles, Being There Can Only Help

THE car gives a hint to my status as a punter. I've got the Romany Rye golf clubs, the Rambo's Hall television set and the Sinndar stereo, but there never was a Mole Board BMW.

The car I do have has acquired a few dents and perhaps I should give them names as well, to symbolise the days when my experience of the turf was less than glorious. The thing is, though, that, in my memory, the good days far outweigh the bad.

There is no corroborating evidence. The test of those who take gambling seriously, they say, is keeping a record of all their bets. I don't have one.

There is a similar test of my own – at 8.30 on a Saturday morning, are you (a) skipping down to the newsagent for your *Racing Post* to check on the morning prices, or (b) staggering around the kitchen nursing a hangover. I have been known to fail this test as well.

For most punters, horserace betting is not really a case of steely resolve in the pursuit of profit. No-one wants to lose, of course, and an astute punter won't have to, but gaining an edge over the oddsmakers and other punters, knowing more than they do and using that information more effectively – these are not things to go into half-heartedly.

Small profit margins and a large turnover; not everyone will enjoy this, even if they prove successful at it. Horserace betting is not, in the long run, about being lucky or unlucky, it is about forming an opinion and testing it, and that is one of its greatest joys.

Having spent much of the last twenty years as a racegoer trying to acquire the important life skill of how to lose with a modicum of good grace, it comes as something of a shock to realise that I must be an optimist. The key is this – there is never a last race.

This maxim is usually referred to, and wisely so, by those urging some restraint in the getting-out stakes, but it has a wider relevance. There may be a losing day, but what is learnt in the process can lead to future profits.

Today's losing horse can be tomorrow's winner and vice versa, and, if the enmities and sentimental attachments of first acquaintance can be put to one side (not always a formality), we should be all the wiser.

The racecourse is the best place to make that acquaintance. The abolition of off-course betting tax and the rise of the person-to-person betting exchanges have diminished its status as the place to get the best returns, but there is no better place to arm yourself for those bets.

In a big race for older horses, the runners are mostly fit and well and their ability is largely established. Look at a field of maidens, however, and what you're looking at is the future, betting material in the long term as well as the short term, because these horses have their careers in front of them.

Trying to predict what that career might bring, perhaps years in advance, is one of the challenges. There could be as much to learn before a race as there is during it.

With terrestrial television increasingly obsessed with arty camera angles, and with daily non-terrestrial racing coverage preferring inane chitchat and action from Brough Park and South Africa, the racecourse has also become the best place to see a race replay.

Unearthing some sort of rationale to my own betting is not that easy, but perhaps there is an attempt to concentrate in two areas;

a) races in which I am familiar with the participants, and/or

b) races in which there is a decent chance of winning. Backing the Wokingham or National winner is not just about the money, is it?

But there really isn't any need to adopt a betting machismo that requires the conquest of every 30-runner handicap. While those races tend to be ruled out, one might rule in plenty of maiden races and novice hurdles in which, after a look at the runners in the parade ring, it is clear that the vast majority of the field have no chance, barring accidents.

Talking of which, the racecourse does also have its hazards and distractions for the punter. While gin and tonics on a summer's day at Goodwood is something close to idyllic, and an experience one might want to share, a day at the races is not always the ideal occasion for the punter who also has some romantic aspiration to attend to.

One newspaper may have called this 'The Sport of Flings', but gadding about arm in arm, hand in hand, is no aid to dashing from the paddock to the bookmakers and then snapping up 9-4 about a 2-1 shot.

And perhaps there is another danger there. It would be sad indeed if you ever had to spend Saturday afternoon trundling round Ikea.

# CHAPTER 7
# IN THE SHOPS

The public face of horserace betting, **JOHN McCRIRICK** is possibly the only racing journalist to have achieved wide recognition outside the sport. A tireless campaigner for the rights of punters everywhere, we could have no better guide to life within the country's betting shops.

## My Guide to Making it Pay from the Bookie's

HAVING overcome shyness and sidled through the door, you will usually be confronted by vast displays of information on banks of television screens and in sporting newspapers displayed around the walls. If not already convinced about what you want to back, this welter of advice will offer the most detailed of clues.

But bear in mind a few gems of advice about off-course betting;

You can bet at starting price (SP) or at the board price displayed on the screens or on the shop's board at the time you place the bet. If taking a board price, make this clear on your slip: it will be authorised by the clerk at the counter, and those are the odds at which (if on a winner) you will be paid.

Be careful to fill out the slip accurately and clearly. Too many disputes about bets arise from confusing or ambiguous instructions and, most frequent of all, mis-spelling. Be especially alert for horses with similar names.

On 2 May 1988, White-Wash (20-1) won a maiden at Warwick and Whitewash (USA) finished sixth at Doncaster at 12-1 . . . both trained by John Dunlop! On 30 June 1994, Averti (USA) ran for Henry Cecil at Yarmouth – one of her opponents was Averti (IRE), trained by William Muir.

On 25 January 2001, Didntcostalotbut took part in a novices' hurdle at Warwick just half an hour before her stablemate Wontcostalotbut ran in a handicap hurdle at the same track. Write down the wrong one and you won't be paid if your choice wins.

Be careful to stake your bet properly, especially in a complicated multiple. A £2 each-way Yankee, for example, will cost you £44. If you get your calculations wrong, stakes on each bet in the multiple will be adjusted proportionally.

Familiarise yourself with the bookmakers' rules. They are not the same in every shop and ignorance could prove very costly. In 1984, Edward Hodson, a Wolverhampton punter, had a 5p Yankee in which all four horses won, at aggregate odds of 3,956,748-1. But instead of a return of not far off £20,000 for his 55p investment, he received just £3,000, his bookie's payout limit. Limits vary from £1,000 to £250,000.

Remember the implications of backing an unnamed favourite in a race. If there are joint-favourites, your stake is halved and placed equally on both, and likewise is divided between co-favourites.

Backers of the unnamed favourite for the Law Society Legal Handicap Hurdle at Hexham in April 1991 had their fingers crossed, but in the event there were seven co-favourites, who went off at 6-1. Six of them filled the first six places, while the seventh was a tailed-off last. A £7 win single on the unnamed favourite in a race like that would, these days, leave you level – £6 for £1 on the 6-1 winner, plus a £1 stake returned. In those days, it would have been a loser off-course, thanks to the 10% tax levied at the time.

For many people, the soul has gone out of betting shops. They have live racing coverage and high-tech processing of bets and information, but many punters yearn for the good old days of fug, babble and genial boardmen, who would double as father confessor or agony aunt (in drag) to the mentally tortured punters. No-one was a better judge of form, or at least reckoned he was, than the charismatic boardman. In my days with the chalk, the regulars soon learned to take no notice of me – just as on Channel Four Racing now!

No-one yearns for the good old days more than I, a founder member of Nostalgia Freaks Inc, but if shops went back twenty years, they'd soon be empty.

And what has not changed is the human side of betting shops. Most punters operate in solitary fashion, studiously making their choices by themselves, rather than engaging in a general discussion of prospects with other customers. But, come the 'off', the entire band are subjected to a communal anguish, from which only a few will emerge as winners.

During the race, different punters react variously. Some yell advice at Pat Eddery or Tony McCoy (so much easier these days, when they can see what those champions are doing 'wrong'), others huddle in corners, desperate for the agony of the race to be over, or pace the floor like expectant fathers, while some just stand or sit impassively. They are all united in the exquisite anxiety and suffering of betting.

That's one thing you can be sure of. Everyone who gambles is a sufferer. Stoically, they endure travesties of fortune. Bad luck is never far away, or so they believe.

Sufferers divide into two breeds. The first strides into his or her betting shop, looks up at the screen or board and, if the horse they've backed isn't in the frame, simply cannot believe it. Quickly, they scan the non-runners; no, it ran. So did it fall, was it disqualified by the Stewards, or even did the wretched jockey forget to weigh in? Their own judgement can't have been at fault – or so they kid themselves.

The second kind of sufferer, the more sensible (can there be such a breed?), glance up at the results and are incredulous if their choice has won.

All the misfortunes that could have befallen it have been overcome. A miracle indeed!

# CHAPTER 8
# INSIDE INFORMATION

WHEN reading or listening to the words of owners, trainers, jockeys or anyone offering 'inside' advice, bear in mind that such people are generally poor tipsters. Owners, even form experts who have become owners, tend to over-rate their own runners.

Trainers, jockeys and anyone connected with a stable may be very familiar with the form of their charges and their well-being, but are unlikely to be so well-informed about the opposition.

In the bad old days, when racing was not perhaps so straight as it is now, when there were no camera patrols keeping a beady eye on the field, it was certainly a benefit to have a 'marked card'.

Nowadays, the average backer has as much information at his disposal as anyone more intimately connected with the sport and, with experience, can use it more objectively and to better effect than an insider could.

Super-sharp trainers will still run a horse over the wrong trip and possibly on adverse ground to get a favourable handicap mark – whatever their critics may say, this practice is entirely above-board, so long as the horse is always given every chance to run to its best. It's up to the punter to spot these ploys and try to get in on the gamble when the horse eventually turns out under ideal conditions.

Even so, unless you're in a position to clarify it, 'inside' information will turn your pockets inside out. Dark horses and well-planned coups may go on but current form is always a much more reliable bet than trying to spot the plot.

Many of the stables who are never likely to have a Group contender opt to rely on a successful coup to stay solvent. Making a study of how such yards campaign their runners can be a fascinating way to pass the time.

Of course, there's precious little in the way of reliable advance information about the runners from a gambling yard. Unfortunately, such connections will always know more about their runners than you.

For that reason, intrigue and chicanery should be hard-pressed to get a walk-on part in your gambling. Your biggest and most frequent bets should be on good horses, produced by trainers who aim for prize money rather than the bookies' money.

Over the next few pages, Ivor Herbert offers an insight into how trainers plot their coups, while John Sexton counsels against listening to anyone who might appear to be offering inside knowledge. Finally, Michael Church weighs in with an hilarious and true tale of unreliable touts – here's hoping that no-one who reads this has ever paid his uncle Albert for information!

---

*A long-serving racing journalist, editor, travel writer, scriptwriter, author, playwright and Cheltenham Gold Cup-winning trainer, IVOR HERBERT has found time for several successful careers. And he's learned a thing or two about betting, along the way . . .*

## Doing the Stable Commission

IGNORE the telly-tosh talked about betting. Fat pundits will tell you after a favourite has gone in, 'Well-backed, you see . . . Ladbrokes knew it would win.'

Ladbrokes' glossy-haired, twinkle-eyed PR man Mike Dillon certainly knows things well ahead of the game in Ireland. His connections with Coolmore and Ballydoyle are long and close. They spin snugly over all of Ireland.

But you'll hear only after hefty wagers (like those on Papillon for the 2000 Grand National) have been struck. And sometimes not 'til they've been landed, with the race won . . .

That's how stable commissions work. The world should not know first. When I was training some good jumpers, we used to place our own wagers with dear old Ted Sturman of Fred Binns, a proper bookmakers of the old school.

Like all bookmakers handling regular stable commissions, he gained valuable information: that a horse was fancied and, by the size of the bet, how much it was fancied – more or less than our average punt. We gained, as all stables gain, the advantage of several points better than starting price, often a considerable gain.

The deal was simple. We would speak early to Ted and undertake not to back the horse elsewhere off-course. Secrecy was all. We mustn't spoil the market.

My then wife, shrewd on form, would go to Ted well before the first race. Ted, registering how strongly we expected to win, could calculate that the horse was exceptionally well, had done a good gallop, schooled brilliantly etc. He then had plenty of time and margin to lay off our bet in the market. The price began to shorten.

In return, he would give us, say, £500 at 10s, £300 at 7s and £200 at 4s, with the horse starting (and quite often winning) at about 3s.

You can assess price movements from the screens. But lots can be mere book-balancing by crafty bookies. You need to be close enough to the ground to know who, from which stable, struck what size of bet with which bookmaker. Outsiders will never know the exact transactions. You must guess.

But here's the twist in the tail, and a moral, too. We used to mount about half a dozen big punts a season when I was training. Four of six would come storming home. We made serious money.

Since I stopped training, I've stopped betting, too. Why? It's obvious; you've got to be right in the game to have the faintest chance of making money.

Don't believe punters who tell you otherwise. Instead, look at the big bookies' colossal profit figures. And beware!

**JOHN SEXTON** is *racing editor of the* Wolverhampton Express & Star *and President of the Horserace Writers & Photographers Association*

## The Only Useful Tip is to Ignore Tips

I guess that, at some time in our racing lives, we have all succumbed to the belief that there is a group of people operating in the sport who have the key to every successful gamble and, if only we could break into that magic circle, our financial worries would be over.

It is a myth that has been perpetuated over the years by deeds of derring-do in the betting ring, of plots hatched in remote manor houses and carried out to the letter, as well as the talk of 'faces' and 'those in the know'. Sorry to disappoint you, but it just isn't true.

Well, that's not quite correct. It's true up to a point. For example, it is true that Barry Hills, for over 30 years one of the top trainers in Britain, got his start thanks to a major bet on the Lincoln Handicap. And it is true that, every day, well-planned gambles are landed. But it is also true that, every day, far more well-planned gambles go astray in greater numbers. So, when you're urged to 'come racing' in the hope of tuning in to the racecourse whispers that will provide you with every winner every day, think again. It just isn't going to happen.

That's not to say there is no value to be had on a racecourse. There is. But, in my experience, the value is in what you see, rather than in what you hear.

As examples of the latter, I like to quote a race at Catterick a few years ago in which I was on good terms with the connections of a number of runners in a nine-horse race, so much so that I was told that no less than five of them were 'good things'. Needless to say, the race was won by one of the other four.

It's much better to use a racecourse for making your own observations and acting on them. The parade ring can be a great source of winners, particularly in two-year-old races, and you should always try to go and look at them.

I have known a few good judges of two-year-olds who made more money out of betting on what they had seen in the parade ring than any amount of 'information' could have brought.

I cannot profess to be a great judge of a two-year-old, but practice does bring improvement and sometimes you see one that even an untrained eye could not help but spot. And they don't always start favourite!

Viewing in the parade ring is, to my mind, one of the most important facets of going racing, although sometimes it can be difficult, particularly at the major meetings when it is physically impossible to view the parade ring, have a bet and still get a good pitch from which to watch the race.

At Cheltenham, Epsom and Royal Ascot, it is often a case of perming any two from three, so my advice would be to do the parade ring and have a bet. And set the video to watch the races in detail when you get home!

But whatever you decided, one thing is certain: you will have more fun on the racecourse than in the fug of the betting shop, so yes, come racing!

---

*MICHAEL CHURCH joined the* Racing Post *as accountant in 1986 and became Special Projects Manager, covering the promotion of racing and greyhound events. He's written a series of tomes on bloodlines and the history of the Turf. The following story is a cautionary tale of commercial tipsters, taken from his latest book,* Ripping Gambling Yarns *(published by Raceform, £12.95).*

## Ace Information

DAD'S brothers, Albert and Henry were always short of money: Albert due to his unsuccessful betting and Henry because the pittance he earned from his gardening job barely covered the rent that Albert charged him for his dilapidated terraced house.

Despite this imbalance, they remained good friends. So much so, that, one day, sitting up at Henry's kitchen table (tea and Woodbines to hand), Albert, reading the adverts in the sporting press, came up with the idea that they could both earn a bit of spare cash by advertising 'confidential racing information.'

At first, Henry thought this a little ironic, since his brother's financial predicament was entirely due to his tenuous understanding of the sport. However, as Albert revealed the details of his scam and the very little capital needed to start-up, Henry, ever susceptible to Albert's influence, warmed to the idea.

'First we put an advert in one of the racing papers – Ace Information sounds the business – then, ask the readers to send us a five shilling postal order for three Saturday advices.'

'Where do we get the information from?' quizzed Henry.

'Easy,' said Albert, eyes twinkling, 'we buy the Sporting Record midweek, pick out three of their tips for the weekend and, as soon as the postal orders come rolling in, we'll send them our special advices – no sweat, no risk, money for old rope.'

'We've still got to put together the advert and write the letters,' worried Henry, aware of his own limitations.

At this stage, Albert hadn't given much thought to the details but, on hearing me chatting to Aunty Mary in the scullery, called out, 'You made the frame in English this term, didn't you Michael?'

'Well, yes, if you count finishing fourth,' I replied cautiously.

'Well then, you can be our secretary,' Albert enthused. And with that, I joined them to work out the details, requesting the expenses necessary to cover the advert, stationery and stamps. It seemed the 'advices' would be handwritten until the brothers became famous and bought a typewriter.

After two weeks, we had received only three postal orders and given no winners. But the third week Albert tipped Cherry Herring, a 9-1 winner at Lingfield, and promptly advertised his success in the next edition of the paper. The response was instant – fourteen postal orders. And the week after, when Assouan (100-30), and Cadet Roussel (20-1), both won on St Leger day, I had to take a day off from school (suffering conveniently from hayfever and asthma), to get more than thirty letters off in time. That evening, I put it to Albert that my increased workload was worth ten bob a week and, wincing slightly, he shook my hand on it.

Later that month, maintaining a handsome level-stakes profit, Albert tipped Eastern Emperor, another big-priced winner. But it was not until I was compiling an advert listing our winners to date that it suddenly hit me. All our tips began with the letters A, C or E . . . ACE.

'So that's why Albert had insisted our service be called Ace Information,' I thought. When I quizzed him on it, he became defensive.

'Would you rather I tipped a string of losers, then, Michael?' he protested. I backed off.

Henry, now with the dry rot repaired in his upstairs bedrooms and a new dart board, said nothing. And although my heart sank at the naivety of it all, Albert's belief in his tipping abilities soared, and the next time I met him he positively glowed.

'I've been checking through my tipping record since we started and I've decided that we should reinvest our profits in our own tips!'

'But what if we lose?' queried Henry, now used to moving freely about in his upstairs bedrooms.

'Lose?' retorted Albert defiantly. 'We'll worry about that when it happens.'

'I think I'll hang on to my ten shillings a week, if that's alright with you, Uncle,' I said.

That weekend and the next, Albert and Henry's reinvestment paid off. Albert was now talking seriously about buying a new fish van, while Henry was tentatively considering a new spade.

Albert now took his dreams a stage further.

'Look Henry, why are we waiting until Saturday to bet, when I can pick three specials every day?'

'But the Sporting Record doesn't come out until Wednesday,' said Henry, as usual not up to Albert's speed.

'Oh, sod the Sporting Record,' Albert snorted, 'I'll pick my own winners.' And he did – all beginning with the letters A, C and E.

Albert was now a regular at Charlie Young's betting room. Alice (Charlie's wife), said he should bring his bed with him, since he was also applying his 'winning system' to the greyhounds at Wimbledon and White City.

The increased size of our tipping adverts, although bringing in more business, coincided with a run of short-priced winners for Albert. And now, having advised his clientele to bet in pounds rather than shillings, he was convinced that it was their money bringing the prices down. Beset by a combination of paranoia and megalomania, he stopped advertising, leaving Henry to his faithful garden and me out of a part-time job.

Albert now entered a crisis. Continually faced with more than one choice of the magic capital letters in a race, he invariably picked the wrong one, and, in desperation, decided to back them all. Tragically, this occurred simultaneously with a complete absence of these letters from the results page. A week later, he was broke.

The following month, while I was playing darts with Henry in his back yard, Albert's round, beaming face appeared over the gate.

'I've got some good news chaps – I know where we went wrong.'

We cautiously put down the darts to listen.

'T – O – P,' he explained, 'Top Information.'

Todman (8-1), Oscar (7-1), Pinkthorn (10-1).

'How about it lads?'

# CHAPTER 9
# FLAT OR JUMPS?

**CHRIS MCGRATH** is racing correspondent with The Times.

## Going a Bit Cool on the Winter Game

PERHAPS it's plain prejudice.

Yes, we've all backed horses that approach the last fence a mile clear, and only the jockey gets over. But we have all winced, equally, as our selections are ambushed by a sudden, mysterious and wholly implacable advantage in the draw.

Even so, the fact remains that nowadays I very seldom bet over jumps. As I say, this may have something to do with other objections, concerning aesthetics or even ethics – with the fact, for instance, that you have to be slightly peculiar to seek profit from the sort of grotesque spectacle that ensues after two exhausted, mud-caked animals kick and slither across the final hurdle.

Such delicacy, of course, should count for nothing with the gambler. We are supposed to be ruthless opportunists. The lord of the jungle does not decline a dinner of raw antelope simply because there is no rowanberry pickle. Yet a rogue streak of logic lurks somewhere beneath my bigotry.

Think about it. Think about all those terrible punting disasters, those teeth-in-the-gutter days when a racehorse sneaks up behind you and rips the pavement from under your feet. Not always a racehorse, mind – often its jockey, sometimes even a bloke innocently driving a tractor round Wolverhampton. Over jumps, these episodes reflect the coarseness of their context. Your bad luck is there for all to see. The demands of the race stretch the runners out like sausages on a butcher's slab.

If they don't win, it is almost always for a conspicuous reason. They cannot jump, or they hate the ground, or they don't stay. Most of all, of course, they don't win because they are irredeemably crappy horses.

On the Flat, however, you can at least try to use your brains. There are many more shades between black and white.

Though modern race analysis is an awful lot more sophisticated than it was even a few short years ago, people are still missing plenty. Spotting bias in the track, whether favouring a certain stretch of ground or a certain style of running, is second nature to the American punter. But his instinct cannot be easily harnessed to the variegation of racecourses in Britain.

In fact, if you try to account for everything – pace bias, pace distribution, draw, going, distance, pedigree, speedfigure profile, stable form – you will go quietly insane. It is impossible. You simply cannot cover all the angles.

Perfect! Because if you can't, nor can anybody else. And that gives you half a chance. You have some room for intellectual manoeuvre.

Jumping form is largely veneer. On the Flat, each race comprises a dozen different layers. You may not win a lot of money, working it out – but you can at least retain a measure of self-respect.

The principles and techniques you learn on the Flat somehow fall to bits the moment you apply them to jumpers. Imagine an eight-runner chase containing four inveterate front-runners. In a Flat handicap, you would immediately put a line through all four and back a hold-up horse. In the chase, however, one of the front-runners will probably just keep going, while the tyres gradually start bouncing off everything else.

On the Flat, moreover, it is much easier to interpret what a trainer is trying to achieve. Jumpers tend to be long-term projects, which is just another way of saying that nobody has any real idea how things are going to turn out.

It is very hard to distinguish between a store horse that needs time, and a store horse that needs to be put in a tin. The impatient cycles of a Flat stable permit far less guesswork.

Over jumps, big-priced winners tend to be flukes. They come looking for you, carrying a big stick. You are seldom pleased to see them. On the Flat, you can get out there and find them.

And I'm telling you that on the level.

# Tips for the Flat

## Group races

With so much racing on these days, more and more punters are, very sensibly, opting to specialise on a particular kind of race. So, should you become a Groupie?

In theory, form lines should never be more reliable than in races at the exalted levels of Group One or Two, contested by well-prepared horses from top yards, with leading jockeys in the saddle.

Just the same, you'll have to be wary of an apparently impressive winner of a Group race or Listed event for which it had been trained for months. A quick reappearance may be no more than an attempt to capitalise.

Don't allow the inevitable publicity to persuade you that this horse is a 'good thing'. Having achieved its connections' ambition, it will now be taking on rivals whose campaigns were specifically planned with this second race in mind.

Such ploys can sometimes pay off but more often this horse is making the market for those who want to back others against it.

Fillies especially tend to be more reliable at the highest level, though paddock judges will always be in the best position to assess whether they're likely to give their best on a certain day.

## Conversely . . . the low life

Like so much in life, sellers ain't what they used to be and punters' lives are further complicated by claimers.

Look out for horses who, having been easy winners at the lowest level, are returning to claimers or sellers after abortive attempts at better races. Especially if they're with the same trainer, they'll be likely to go close.

Have a look at anything that's recently been bought or claimed by trainers with good records in such races.

Respect gambles on unraced juveniles in sellers, which often pay off. Connections sometimes go for this option when they have a youngster capable of nearly winning a modest maiden, but which is rated a certainty against 'plating' opposition.

It's more profitable for them to land a quick coup and risk losing out at the subsequent auction than to fail narrowly in the maiden and then have their horse's ability immediately exposed.

The biggest problem facing the punter in claimers is how to assess those 'well in' at the weights. Trainers sometimes run horses in claimers who have been decent performers in the past, perhaps because their charge has deteriorated physically or mentally.

Carrying a light weight, because a lowish claiming price has been set by connections, such a horse may appear to be a good thing, but can it really beat claiming-class types who run consistently to form and win in their turn, or who may have been laid out for a coup in the race?

Certain trainers farm claimers, especially in midsummer. Come September, though, with more and more horses being dropped in class, you'll have to tread carefully. The market may be your best guide to whether or not a horse has retained enough of its former ability to win such an event.

Equine psychology is also worth considering. Some horses are happier dominating their inferiors than when having to fight their corner against rivals of similar ability.

In any claimer, the horse with the best exposed current form will take all the beating. Confidence among less-exposed types will hopefully be reflected in the market.

## The break factor

It used to be the case that juveniles would need at least ten days' rest after their racecourse debuts before they could do themselves justice again. In recent years, this trend has been bucked by several successful stables.

Beware of any horse that runs well after a lengthy absence – it could easily go backwards next time and should be avoided unless having had another decent break, or unless it's in the hands of a trainer you respect.

Juveniles and three-year-olds that would be hard-pressed to win a maiden of any consequence are often given an easy time in their first three runs, for which they're unfancied by connections and nearly always run as badly as expected.

They're then given a break before being campaigned in nurseries or handicaps, when their apparently poor form will allow them to race with a favourably light weight. Look out for such horses taking part in their first handicaps after some time off.

## Quick returns

Note also runners that have been good winners of apprentice races, turning out quickly in 'open' handicaps without a penalty and before reassessment.

Similarly, convincing handicap winners who return under a penalty, before the handicapper's had a chance to reassess them, can prove worth following.

## Respect experience

Experience is at a premium in juvenile and three-year-old sprint maidens during the first two months of each Flat season, especially if the ground has been wet and the winter severe.

Two-year-olds in particular are raced over sprint distances, where a brisk start can be critically important. Youngsters having their second or third run are more likely to break well and can provide a value bet at the expense of a well-backed newcomer.

Even if a debutant starts well, he may be unable to hold his position through greenness and, even if he can run on in the closing stages, can be left with too much to do.

Among the three-year-olds, good each-way bets can be found if you note contestants reverting to five and six-furlong maiden races after taking part in handicaps, especially if they have the ground and the draw in their favour.

On many occasions, the market allows you to support such a horse against an unraced favourite and cover your bet with a forecast, to be second to the market leader.

## Course and distance

Be wary of supporting horses over any distance other than their proven trip. Prize money and the prestige of a famous race often seduce contenders into taking part when conditions are adverse.

With commercial breeders ostracising the out-and-out stayer, many genuine Cup horses have had their hearts broken taking on middle-distance opposition in an attempt by connections to boost their charge's stud value.

In reverse, the pure sprinter is often tried at trips around a mile, only being allowed to revert to their natural distance once they've palpably failed to stay on one or more occasions.

Similarly, milers are tried over ten furlongs, twelve-furlong specialists are put back to ten furlongs and so on.

It's up to the punter to ensure that he concentrates on backing an animal running over its optimum trip. When making such decisions, the nature of the track must be taken into account – stiff tracks will require more stamina than normal for any given distance, while the opposite is true of easy courses. Every backer with aspirations to semi-seriousness must know the layout of any racecourse on which he's punting, and the individual demands it makes on the horses.

## Short and sweet

Two factors can determine the result of a seemingly intimidating sprint handicap with up to 30 runners;

1. the draw
2. sprinters in form; they can retain and improve upon their form and keep ahead of the handicapper. They also stand more racing within shorter periods, so note winners out again quickly before reassessment.

A sprinter in form, with ground and draw favourable, should be kept on your side. This is more important than actual handicapping. A sprinter in form can offset a weight disadvantage; equally, one out of form may well fail to capitalise on a lenient mark.

The daunting obstacle for punters in a sport with no obstacles is the draw. With stalls positioning and watering, it has become even more decisive in determining results. Any 'known' advantage must be turned to your advantage.

I have always considered the draw to be of even more importance in competitive races with eight or more runners. Here, closely handicapped contestants will profit from any bonus.

'Softer' events, such as maidens or races with a runner outstanding on paper are not so dependent on a good draw, though it certainly helps.

## The market as a guide to youngsters

In juvenile or maiden races, respect the chance of any horse which opens at a short price, even if it then drifts. Its initial position in the market must stem from good work at home.

Watch its performance carefully. Should it fail through inexperience, ill luck in running or lack of fitness, be sure to note its next appearance – especially if it's in the hands of a good trainer.

The market can be misleading. Once there's been an early move for the 'dark' prospect, forcing it down to short odds, money will come for the more exposed runners from those looking for a bit of value. It doesn't mean there's a lack of confidence behind the favourite.

Backing juvenile favourites blind in the first quarter of the season used to be a profitable system; no longer. Indeed, I can't ever recall a time when there were so many open and indecisive betting heats in this kind of race.

Even so, when there's a favourite at 5-4 or shorter with nothing seriously backed to beat it, don't oppose it lightly unless you've a specific reason for doing so.

## Defying their elders

For whatever reason, three-year-olds can now succeed against their elders in handicaps at an earlier stage in the season than was the case in the past.

This is especially true in middle-to-long distance events, as the youngsters have more improvement in them when stepping up in trip. They do not hold this advantage against older sprinters and are up against it until after Royal Ascot.

This observation is in keeping with what happens in Group and condition events, which also favour older contestants until mid-season, though a classy three-year-old can buck this trend.

## Changing discipline

In Flat handicaps, you must note horses which have shown markedly improved form over hurdles, particularly in the opening weeks of the Flat season.

Perhaps more importantly, watch out for horses which have rediscovered their form on the All-Weather surfaces and then return to the Flat, running in handicaps under their old rating, which may be amazingly lower than their rating on sand.

You can check the difference in such ratings in the *Racing Post* or one of the other trade papers. I've seen a plethora of winners in recent seasons from following this system and feel it's only a matter of time before a ruling is introduced to offset the advantage. Be sure to benefit from the current rules while they last. It's well worth the time necessary to explore this idea. Prices can be good and, in many instances, racecourse fitness is an added advantage they hold over their purely turf rivals.

# Tips for the Jumps

## The National Hunt season

National Hunt racing today has changed to such an extent that I feel it offers its soundest betting opportunities within the boundaries of the Flat season.

The period between mid-October and New Year sees a plethora of novice and juvenile prospects appearing, with varied reputations and price-tags. We're presented with ex-Flat horses, including some of Irish, French and German origin, together with 'National Hunt Flat' horses from Britain and Ireland – and, as if this were not enough, non-thoroughbreds from France. This latter type has come into vogue since it became clear that many such horses are of above-average ability.

At exactly the same time of year as we're seeing these new stars for the first time, many hurdlers are going novice chasing.

It all comes together to form a nightmare scenario for punters until Cheltenham, or until monsoon conditions have abated.

One redeeming feature of our old British winter was the paucity of racing during January and February, due to the frost and snow. This inclement weather at least offered some respite to the horses and, even more important, the courses, too many of which can now resemble a bog, taxing both runners and punters alike.

Something I've noticed during the past season is that several highly-regarded French imports have at last found winning form, when having been given a short break and returning to race on a decent surface.

This is possibly due to one of two factors. Either they were not acclimatised beforehand, or they had shown form on bottomless ground in France (where such a surface is continually prevalent), but were basically crying out for good ground.

## Swapping codes

My most important jumps message is this; scour the novice chases for hurdlers making their debuts. Don't wait for them to gain experience – first time up is the time to catch them.

From mid-October until Christmas, there are possibly too many in a race to play successfully, though not always and so many times there is a previous novice chase winner with a penalty to 'make' your market and your payday.

I have frequently seen jaded hurdlers going for it first time out over fences, never putting a foot wrong, beating a favourite with experience, only to 'think' about it on their next outing and succumb to another debutant chaser. Any tipster who writes that some horse 'is making his chasing debut and is probably best watched on this occasion' has not been at this delightful game as long as I have.

Having said that, ex-pointers should be avoided when taking on regulation fences for the first time, even if they've been successful in their previous exploits. A lack of speed can often hold them back and they shouldn't be supported until they've proven their worth.

Hurdlers can win over fences despite being half-fit after a long lay-off, while a chaser can also return to win in similar circumstances.

However, for any type of horse to win over hurdles when backward is rare, unless the opposition is poor.

It has become increasingly in vogue to 'pop' a hurdler straight into a handicap chase. Success has encouraged several trainers to do this and prices can be good. The handicapper has no idea where to put such horses and usually errs on the side of leniency – though you'll get many losers by following such types, the prices of the winners should prove worthwhile when it goes right.

Also note ex-hurdlers in novice handicap chases, as debutants can be in on more favourable terms than in an ordinary novice chase. A hurdler with useful form getting weight from moderate novice chasers is worth a risk bet at fair odds.

## The best race for the punter . . .

This is, without doubt, the ordinary novice hurdle, the best betting vehicle of any horserace. Professional backers love these events, while bookies fear them.

Experience is at a premium, so there's little form to study, but what form there is is nearly always reliable. Those dropped in class are particularly worth following.

I would rarely support an unraced novice hurdler, however, even one with useful Flat form. To justify my faith, it would have to be from a top stable and unopposed by anything with a remote chance on its hurdling form.

Even in such rare instances, prices will be unattractive, except possibly for pool purposes. Keep in mind also that it is harder, these days, for a novice to run up a sequence of wins, thanks to the penalties that they incur along the way and to changes in race conditions.

## . . . and the worst

Easily the worst race for the average punter is the National Hunt Flat race, or 'bumper'.

Any strong market move should be respected, but racecourse form is either absent or unreliable. Overall, such races are best left alone.

Unfortunately, such contests feature at the end of the card and can tempt the desperate and compulsive gambler into having a crack at getting out of trouble. Here, you have no Flat form to guide you and little idea of how to evaluate winners carrying penalties.

Anyone taking the time to study the breeding of contestants for such a race will probably find one or two classically-bred types from a good yard. If you know the reason that such horses weren't raced on the Flat (perhaps because they were backward or failed the stalls test), then you may have a bet.

More trouble ensues when bumper runners graduate to hurdles. Many don't transmit their form immediately and anyone who tells you he can align their form with hurdlers in open novice races is far too clever to be taken seriously!

## Up-and-coming jockeys

As soon as the most promising amateurs and conditional jockeys emerge, have them riding for you.

This is more important over obstacles than on the Flat. Outside rides should be carefully noted and, in races confined to their status, their expertise is worth a few pounds in the saddle, with their claim invaluable in open handicaps.

## Distance Specialists

Two and a half miles is the tricky distance, both over fences and hurdles.

The genuine specialists at this trip will generally hold the call over two and three-milers being raised and dropped to the distance, especially when ground conditions are not extreme and the course is neither overly sharp or stiff.

## Unexposed types

Note hurdlers in their first runs in handicaps. Analyse their form in novice events and that of their trainer, plus any interesting riding arrangements.

Remember that a horse's form might read '000' but, over hurdles, especially on heavy ground, such form figures need not denote a lack of ability. Easing down when beaten is common, while just one mistake can be enough to knock a horse out of the frame, even if it had been running well up to that point.

Novice chasers often get into 'open' handicaps with a lenient weight, where, time and time again, their youth can allow them to outspeed their experienced opponents.

## Short-priced chasers

It is sheer madness to back a chaser at a short price at any level.

Before the flood of racing that now engulfs us, punters were starved for choice during the winter and could not be blamed for betting at odds-on over fences but today there are many better opportunities every week.

So much can happen during the course of a steeplechase. The proven jumper, always thought to be a reliable conveyance, can come to grief or meet trouble in running.

At odds-on, you'll back many winners but in the long run you'll lose money and suffer a lot of unnecessary stress.

## The importance of experience

Try to refrain from supporting hurdling debutants. Again, though you'll miss winners, you'll also avoid many losers.

I can't over-stress the importance of experience in this sphere. So many Flat horses fail to make the transition, or take time to learn, yet they often carry big reputations with them into the winter game that shortens up their price on their debut.

A Flat racer whose form was over trips short of 1m2f will probably have stamina problems in a 2m hurdle race. Equally, horses needing 2m or so to show their best on the Flat will need 2m4f over hurdles.

Avoid hard-pulling hurdlers and anything that refuses to settle after its second race over timber – they continually beat themselves.

The newcomers are most vulnerable on soft ground or worse, while sharp tracks and those with closely-grouped obstacles also find them out.

## Juvenile hurdles

These have become less competitive and offer poor value for the spectator until the Triumph Hurdle trials. In contrast, the Triumph itself has now become so competitive, with many horses having gained cheap reputations through an avoidance policy, that it has lost any appeal, betting-wise. Too many of the runners are in the deep end for the first time.

Hurdlers with winning form before November used to get caught out after that time but can now capitalise on their experience into January, so long as the ground doesn't deteriorate greatly.

'Talking' horses abound in these races. Rather than support them blindly, watch and wait for winning form. Remember that heavy ground over hurdles in winter can be rather more testing than the equivalent ground on the Flat.

The juvenile hurdler with some fair maiden form can produce a bet when taking on its elders in all-aged novice events from January. The weight-for-age scale is definitely in its favour.

A good conditional rider also adds to the advantage and such a booking should not be overlooked.

## Last season's juveniles

Four-year-olds from the previous season's top crop find life extremely difficult the following year, especially when carrying penalties for a Grade One win.

Few of the past Triumph Hurdle contenders have subsequently cut much ice – it's a race that seriously taxes its young competitors, both physically and mentally. With many going on to Aintree after an inadequate break for recovery, it's usually those four-year-olds who, for whatever reason, have been spared such campaigns that go on to shine later in their careers.

One of my tried and tested systems is to follow maiden juvenile and novice hurdlers early in the following season. Their experience is a powerful weapon and they often run up sequences before the season's new novices catch them up.

## The French influence

French-breds are back in force but, for some hurdlers bought in France to be brought over here, acclimatisation can be a problem.

I appreciate that advising a watching brief can cause irritation, but then ninety five per cent of all races should be ignored for betting purposes, though they must all be noted with regard to the future.

If you must play, pay particular attention to the ground on which they have won or performed well in the past.

## Claimers and conditions sellers

As with the Flat, the following three questions will allow you to sort good betting prospects from bad in the lowest class of race. Is your fancy . . .

a) . . . fit, fancied and expected to run to its form?

b) . . . fully exposed, with no possibility of improvement and therefore vulnerable against horses of hitherto unknown quality?

c) . . . on the downgrade, with physical and temperamental defects becoming more obvious with each run?

As with the Flat, some horses revert to claimers with success, preferring to dominate their inferiors than to compete against their equals on handicap terms.

The selling handicap is strictly strychnine, while juvenile non-handicap sellers and claimers are also open to turn-ups, especially when the field is large and made up of lightly-raced, poor-quality animals.

Selling and claiming chases are mercifully few and far between, generally contested by old potboilers and ungenuine sorts, though a clear favourite favoured by the race conditions will oblige more often than not.

## Hunter chases

These are not the races they were. Novice events apart, they've become an excuse to postpone the retirement of ex-handicappers, well past their prime.

The established top hunter chasers with no runs under Rules have, in most instances, formed a successful rapport with their riders, are safe jumpers and run to their form, provided conditions are in their favour.

Most hunter chases can be narrowed down easily, with the greatest proportion being won by the first or second favourite. However, too many odds-on shots have been beaten in recent years and the races in which pros can operate with success are now much fewer.

It's not easy to compare point-to-point form with hunter chase form and, when an outsider does win, you'd require second sight to have predicted its victory.

The race summary in the racing press can be invaluable. The form figures may show a string of point-to-point wins but the form may, in fact, amount to little. It's also important to learn something about the riders in this sphere, with many of the amateurs regularly putting up overweight.

A genuine odds-on favourite with current form, ground, distance and rider all acceptable can be used as a banker in pools bets. Even so, unless you're at the track or have intimate knowledge of 'points' form, give these races a miss.

Paddock inspection can be helpful – don't expect permit holders to produce their charges in peak racing condition on a seasonal debut.

## Watch the clock

Pay attention to the times of juvenile and novice hurdle races, comparing the times of any such races that get divided. Compare them also with the times achieved by more experienced rivals over the same trip at that meeting.

It's not hard to use a rough comparison to get an idea of the relative merit of each race.

## Familiarity breeds success

One of the advantages of the winter game is that you get a much better chance to get to know the horses. Unlike Flat racers, the most successful of whom can have only a handful of runs before being retired to stud, jumpers typically turn up at the track year after year.

This is just as well, since it's also highly important with jump racing to know each horse's preference, in terms of ground, course, distance, jumping ability and, most critically of all, the time of the season when they usually hit peak form.

Some need runs to get fit, others go best when fresh.

If you don't have the time to analyse every runner every day in this way, then you'll have to specialise. If you're betting, it's better to have an intensive knowledge of one part of horseracing than a smattering of knowledge about everything.

Those paid to give you a comprehensive information service should know it all – it's their profession, not yours, so pick their brains for the price of a paper.

## Profit from trainers' errors

In many cases, these are precipitated by desperate owners but I've never seen so many badly-placed and over-raced horses as I have in the last five years.

Too many jumpers are being raced on unsuitable going and on unsuitable courses. This is where the sharp backer can profit, if he knows his form.

It's pointless criticising trainers who appear to lack placing ability, persistently running horses over the wrong trip or on adverse ground – instead, profit from their mistakes. They'll be making a market for you in some races, providing an opportunity you shouldn't miss.

Of course, it's so much easier to ride from the stands and train from the armchair but, if you want to curtail your losses and turn them into a profit, you're going to have to trust *your* judgement rather than that of the trainer.

## Out in front

If I back a favourite over hurdles, I want it to be given a positive ride. So much can go wrong when a horse is held up.

'Stylists' look good when producing their mounts from the last to win cleverly, gaining plaudits from members of the press and leniency from the handicapper. But, in common with most punters, I hold that the best horse on paper, if fit and experienced and not needing to be held up, should be in the front rank throughout. From there, it can capitalise on its hurdling ability, get first run and let its opponents make mistakes while trying to make up ground.

In a slowly-run race, those sitting off the pace can come there cruising, only to blunder at one of the final flights, allowing the leader to pinch a winning lead.

Positive tactics win more races than they lose – favour horses and jockeys likely to employ them.

## Whatever the Racing . . .

### Play a Nap hand

The *Racing Post* runs a competition for the tipsters of the national press, which they call the 'Naps table'. Each tipster nominates one tip every day (the 'Nap') and moves up or down the table according to the return generated by a notional £1 staked on each of their Naps.

Usually about fifty or sixty tipsters take part in the competitions, of which there are two every year – one during the jumps season and one during the Flat.

Scanning the table towards the end of each season provides an insight into what will happen to most people who bet every day – around two-thirds of these full-time tipsters will be running a loss on their selections.

But, as the competition progresses towards the business end, it's always worth taking note of the Naps picked out by those at the head of affairs. These selections will have been chosen with the utmost care and after plenty of research.

Should one of them propose something obscure at a minor meeting, you'd be well-advised to keep it on your side.

Professionals with a gun to their head can turn in some inspired performances and you can benefit.

### Find out the state of the ground

This plays a critical role in deciding the outcome of races. An apparent advantage of 7lb can be nullified by adverse going.

Form can work out at any time, so long as ground conditions remain constant, but, when 'God waters his gardens', it's the bookmakers whose prayers are answered.

As if it weren't hard enough to pick a winner, punters have the changeable British weather to cope with, while artificial watering can sometimes leave a fast strip giving a marked advantage to those trainers and jockeys who walk the course properly.

Most horses have a marked preference for one kind of ground or another, so the state of the ground is all-important. That's why the period from mid-May to mid-September is generally the best time for the backer, with the going generally on the fast side, leading to consistent performances and reliable form.

If we're to believe the scientists, however, seasonal weather patterns are changing and it does seem that more summer meetings suffer from sudden, ground-changing downpours. Punters must now keep a weather eye on the forecast, when planning their forecasts!

All too frequently, the official state of the going fails to tell anything like the whole story. Note the finishing times of the early races, with a view to making your own assessment before playing the rest of the card. Clockwatchers in the racing press can offer a priceless insight after day one of a meeting at a top track, so look out for their articles.

A horse may have several pounds in hand on paper form but still be a no-hoper if the ground turns against it. Knowledge of your fancy's preference is essential if you want to avoid expensive disappointments.

## Take it easy at the festivals

The big meetings offer excitement and a multitude of betting opportunities. Nowadays, just like Christmas, they're over-hyped well in advance, with the betting shops doing their best to ensure that their customers indulge in spending sprees.

Am I being a killjoy? Well, possibly, but to enjoy these occasions to the full, it may be best to keep a watchful eye on your outgoings.

The moment a race is described as 'competitive', the warning signs are in neon. Naturally, prices are good and more readily obtained at the big festival meetings, but, with most of the competitors trained to the minute and too closely-matched for betting in comfort, a winning run for any one punter will be hard to achieve.

Whilst others are spending their time and money attempting to solve these equine conundrums, spend your time saving on expense, watching and analysing results and keeping your powder dry for easier opportunities. These meetings provide vital formlines for the immediate future.

Your biggest bets should be in races with as few 'live' runners as possible.

## Current form matters

I maintain that, all year round, current form is the prerequisite to successful punting.

Only support horses, trainers and riders in top form, combined with favourable ground and ideal course and distance – that way, at least you'll be giving yourself a fair chance of holding your own.

This may seem trite but it's as important to recognise the importance of current form as it is to understand the meaning of value. It'll also help you avoid optimistic punts on some animal that 'must have a chance if finally returning to form here.'

## Learn from your mistakes

One must profit from past results. After a hard-to-take loser, console yourself with this thought – it's much more productive to decipher why your horse has lost than waste time gloating over one that has won.

Is your loser worth backing again next time? Or was it simply your error to over-estimate it?

For those who only bet occasionally and rationally, giving the loser a second chance can sometimes recoup losses (though you must always check with yourself that you're not 'chasing') but you should restrict such second bites to horses running again in the same type of race against similar opposition.

## Follow the amateurs

If one of the top amateurs is on the form pick, then you've got a reliable bet. The odds won't be great but, especially in non-handicaps, this system will stand you in good stead.

Unfortunately, many such races have been turned into handicaps over the years, making them much less appetising.

## Weigh up the competition

The more experienced you are as a punter, the easier it becomes to tell whether a race is competitive or soft. Eventually, you'll be able to do so by just glancing through the overnight declarations and riding arrangements.

Ability to make this judgement, and to tell how many 'live' runners there are in a race, is a vital starting point when you're deciding where and when to bet. When you're entering a Jackpot or Placepot, you need this ability in order to sensibly structure your perm.

If you've pinpointed a soft race, a short-priced favourite might suddenly seem to offer some value.

Learn which trainers are likely to have their runners ready first time out. Learn also which trainers commonly produce runners that need at least one racecourse outing to attain peak fitness. Keep an eye on which yards are in and out of form.

Such factors will help you eliminate a number of runners – what you're left with is the list of serious contenders.

## Catch the cast-offs

Several trainers have a good record with cast-offs from other yards and horses transferred to them from the sales or by dissatisfied owners.

Putting it bluntly, a good trainer can improve or rejuvenate an animal from a lesser yard and exploit its low handicap mark.

## Pace matters

You don't have to be a serious student of the clock to benefit from it.

For example, it's easy to compare the times achieved by the winners of different races over the same course and distance, thereby gaining an insight into the relative worth of the form.

Be careful when comparing races that were run more than a few days apart, as ground conditions may well have been significantly different. For this reason, the most useful comparison is between the times achieved by the winners of each leg of a divided race.

A slow-run race developing into a sprint after the turn for home is unlikely to produce reliable form – noting how the time compared with the standard time for the track will alert you to such bad guides. Proximity may flatter several of the runners, misleading less well-informed punters when those horses reappear.

Don't get carried away by times recorded on fast ground. Even moderate performers can record impressive times on ground like a pavement, particularly with a following wind.

The danger in a fast-run race, especially on softish ground, is that moderate performers, dropped out, will keep on at one pace when those fighting out the finish have got tired. Don't over-rate such horses.

This kind of thing happens a lot at undulating tracks like Epsom and Brighton. Note the form, but don't rely on it until it's been confirmed.

## Let's see that again

The ability to watch replays at your leisure is a great asset. Watch and record as much racing as you can, especially informative are juvenile races at important meetings.

When re-running a race, don't just watch the principals fighting out the finish. Look for horses running on or suddenly dropping back through the field, anything being fiercely ridden out to little effect and anything that does well under tender handling.

Be sure you know what the evidence means. You may be looking at a horse that's being prepared for a handicap mark, or a drop in class to a seller or claimer . . . or you may just be looking at a horse with a fragile physique that packs up under pressure.

Some particularly skilled riders don't appear to be doing a great deal, yet are in fact getting every ounce of effort from their mounts.

You'll often find that you didn't catch the whole story at first telling, especially if you had eyes only for the one carrying your money.

Using replays together with the close-up comments in the form book and the racing press, it's not difficult to teach yourself to analyse a race and you can reap the rewards from the bookies.

Try to watch instant replays in the betting shops.

## Open your eyes to blinkers

Twenty years ago, with fewer horses in training, it often paid to give a chance to something wearing blinkers for the first time. Though applying them could be a bit of a drastic tactic, and very hit or miss, it produced many long-priced winners.

Some horses need blinkers to get them to concentrate and run to their best, while less-genuine sorts may respond to them only once. Several trainers blinker lazy horses to sharpen them up at home, but then leave them off at the track.

If you know your trainers, you'll be able to spot the ones for whom blinkers are a last throw of the dice and therefore unlikely to have any beneficial effect. Others equip their horses with the blinds when the stable's going through a quiet patch. These are desperation tactics – blinkers/visors don't rekindle fatigue or counter a viral infection.

Streetwise trainers can get a horse's handicap mark down by removing the blinkers until a favourable time.

Visors and tongue straps further complicate matters, so that it's nowadays nonsensical to blindly follow first-time wearers of headgear. Even so, you need to be alive to how they're being used.

## Know your subject

Knowledge is everything. To beat the bookies, you must therefore know everything. Know your racecourses, what draw biases they exhibit, what ground changes have given an advantage to which part of the course, what kind of horse will cope best with it.

You must know your horses, your trainers, your jockeys, your press and know them well enough to see past the hype and tell the over-rated from the under-rated.

Get to know trainers from television and their press interviews. You must be able to discern the optimist from the realist. As you become more involved, you may become aware of a bias in your punting against certain trainers, but try to retain your flexibility – and don't oppose them when they hit form.

Read the racing press carefully and listen attentively to what you're told but always make sure you're backing your own judgement, not someone else's. Pay special attention to yesterday's results, close-ups, reports and tips from the gallops watchers.

Note interviews with trainers on their strings. Retain copies of results and invest in an annual form book.

Unless you're confident that you can compare British form with form from overseas, don't bet on races held outside the UK. Try to resist betting on any other sport – racing in Britain today gives you more than enough to keep you totally involved in your spare time. The bookmakers would like nothing better than for you to become distracted.

## *Draw your own conclusions*

What you contribute to the betting shop's profit is up to you. Believe me, you'll need more than your wits, thorough turf knowledge and a level head to show a regular profit at the present time.

# CHAPTER 10
# TAKING A FRESH APPROACH

**JOHN WHITLEY** *is the founder of Racing Research, which publishes Computer Racing Form and Computer Chasing Form. Twice a year, he causes controversy by publishing his updated computerised assessment of the relative ability of British jockeys. Here, he discusses the method behind that assessment.*

### A Hard-headed Look at a Muddle-headed Industry

ACCORDING to a very successful racehorse trainer, 'In horseracing, bullshit beats brains every time.' That might be putting it a bit strongly but there is certainly the odd person in racing who could generously be described as scientifically challenged.

One or two of these characters appear to inhabit a different world in which the most basic scientific laws are unknown and the favoured method of argument is by assertion and rhetoric, rather than the more tedious processes of reasoning.

Racing Research is a business supplying analysis of race results to people who bet in the real world. As such, we find a real-world approach to be the most advisable. If a method or a piece of racing wisdom conflicts with scientific or mathematical sense, we discard it.

Others start with a different set of tools. In the US, one well-known speed figure compiler is evidently unencumbered by much scientific baggage. For twenty years or so, his system of speed figures featured zero-gravity, unexplained discontinuous changes in going allowances and no allowance for the progressive physical development of immature racehorses. Recently, after an analysis conducted on the US racing database, he has concluded that an increase in weight slows a horse down. His findings essentially confirm Newton's work.

At Racing Research, we have developed mathematical models to produce several types of rating, including performance figures for jockeys.

I realised a long time ago that no-one genuinely knew how to assess jockeys in terms of their actual contribution to the partnership with the horse, as opposed to the visual impression they created.

It occurred to me that we had a computer handicapping system with ratings assigned to almost every horse/jockey performance, so we could look at how each horse had performed, in terms of our form ratings, under its different riders.

There was a huge amount of data for the busiest riders, so that variations due to distance, going and so on would virtually cancel out. From all this data, figures for each rider could be derived by a straightforward mathematical process.

The figures produced are an accurate measure of how horses have run, in terms of our form ratings, for the rider relative to other riders.

Some people claim to be able to rank jockeys by riding merit. When I have asked them how they do it, they generally admit that they just rely on a visual impression and have no idea of the true effect that one rider has on the performance level of horses compared to other riders.

Rating the performance of the horse/jockey combination (a job generally considered difficult enough to be left to specialists) is just one stage in the more complex task of extracting the jockeys' relatively small contributions, which are masked by the horses' much greater contribution. Curiously, some in the racing fraternity believe they can do this more complex job in their head.

Traditionally, the worth of a jockey has been assessed largely by his place in each year's jockey championship. Yet this statistic suffers from many biases, including two major ones. These are;

1) jockeys have widely different totals of mounts and

2) the allocation of mounts in each race is most unequal, in terms of the winning chance of each horse.

Given the scale of these two biases, any statistician would reject the 'championship' as virtually useless in identifying the best jockeys. This is precisely the sort of situation for which the phrase 'lies, damn lies and statistics' was made.

These biases are absent from our jockey figures – we explain clearly what the figures are based on and what they represent. From conversations with our subscribers, I have found that they generally value our figures very highly and value 'expert opinion' on jockeys very lowly, while preferring that the general betting public are guided by the experts.

On our figures, Ray Cochrane was undoubtedly the best professional jockey riding in Britain. It's a pity that some of the 'racing professionals', whose judgements on jockeys have as much substance as the Emperor's New Clothes, never realised how good he was.

The table overleaf shows the annual performance figures over the years 1991-2000 for all jockeys who appeared in at least eight of our annual listings and had an average figure of 11.0 or more. I should emphasize that the annual figures are not exactly comparable from year to year – the level of each annual list is determined by setting its mean to 10.

| Mean | | 1991 | 1992 | 1993 | 1994 | 1995 | 1996 | 1997 | 1998 | 1999 | 2000 |
|---|---|---|---|---|---|---|---|---|---|---|---|
| 12.7 | R Cochrane | 12.3 | 12.7 | 12.9 | 12.1 | 12.7 | 13.0 | 11.9 | 12.8 | 12.8 | 13.8 |
| 12.3 | L Dettori | 11.9 | 12.4 | 12.2 | 12.1 | 12.8 | 12.5 | 12.7 | 12.3 | 12.1 | |
| 12.0 | K Fallon | 10.4 | 12.4 | 11.3 | 12.2 | 12.8 | 12.4 | 12.5 | 11.8 | 12.3 | 11.4 |
| 11.9 | M Roberts | 13.0 | 12.1 | 12.6 | 12.0 | 11.1 | 11.1 | 12.5 | 11.5 | 12.3 | 11.2 |
| 11.9 | J Reid | 12.9 | 12.0 | 11.8 | 12.1 | 12.6 | 11.9 | 11.8 | 11.8 | 10.5 | 11.1 |
| 11.7 | T Quinn | 11.8 | 11.8 | 11.3 | 12.3 | 12.2 | 12.6 | 11.0 | 11.5 | 11.5 | 11.2 |
| 11.5 | D Holland | 10.3 | 11.6 | 10.6 | 11.4 | 11.0 | 11.2 | 12.3 | 12.4 | 11.5 | 12.7 |
| 11.4 | J Fortune | 10.5 | 9.9 | 11.2 | 11.7 | 12.5 | 11.6 | 11.4 | 11.8 | 12.0 | 11.7 |
| 11.4 | K Darley | 11.1 | 12.7 | 12.1 | 11.7 | 10.6 | 11.5 | 12.1 | 10.7 | 10.4 | 10.6 |
| 11.4 | J Weaver | | 11.3 | 10.1 | 12.3 | 12.4 | 12.3 | 12.5 | 11.2 | 9.7 | 10.9 |
| 11.2 | P Robinson | | 11.4 | 11.0 | 10.9 | 10.0 | 11.5 | | 11.7 | 11.8 | 10.9 |
| 11.1 | M Hills | 11.0 | 11.0 | 10.9 | 10.5 | 10.9 | 10.4 | 11.5 | 10.9 | 11.3 | 11.1 |

These figures measure how horses have responded to the rider, compared to other riders, in terms of our collateral form ratings. They are a measure of the effect of the rider on his mounts.

Statistics such as number of winners, percentages, prize money, big race wins and so on are a different matter. All these are almost totally dependent on the mounts – their quality, in terms of winning chance, and quantity.

The mounts a jockey gets depend entirely on how the jockey is perceived by the people who assign the mounts. That perception is largely dependent on these statistics – it's a circular process.

This explains why the outstanding rider of the last ten years in Britain, on our figures, never won the official jockeys' championship. Ray Cochrane finished top of our annual lists six times in that period, including the last three seasons when he was riding. He retired at the peak of his powers.

**GRAHAM WHELDON** *started a column called 'Sprintline', about the effect of the draw at courses around Britain, in* Raceform On Saturday, *before moving with it to the* Racing & Football Outlook. *His collected thoughts on the subject are published in his book,* Sprintline 2002 *(published by Raceform, £9.99).*

## Where They Start is Key to Where They'll Finish

TO start off, I'm going to hold up my hands and say that I am not the original Mr Draw – I was sort of nurtured on to draw biases and sprint handicaps in my days at Coral's head office, by a well-known modern-day professional punter who spent as much time sampling the delights of Marks & Spencer's custard slices as he did studying form.

As far as I'm concerned, if there were no draw biases at British courses, there would be no point betting on racing. I'd give it up and stick to punting American Football and the Eurovision Song Contest.

Everything I back revolves around a horse's draw, either in today's race, or in previous contests, particularly so the latter. To use an example from last year, the *Racing Post*'s Tom Segal almost pulled off a major 'Pricewise' coup at Ascot with Lady Bear in the Mail On Sunday Final, but she was beaten by her draw, finishing fourth despite easily doing best of the group to race down the centre of the course, having been backed from 66-1 into 20-1.

Less than six months later, Lady Bear reappeared at Doncaster under identical conditions – namely over a straight mile, on soft ground and off the same handicap mark. This time, however, she had the best draw, and she easily won the Spring Mile at 10-1.

It's amazing how often this sort of thing happens. Horses are such creatures of habit, a fact upon which fellow contributor Craig Thake bases his entire approach. Give a horse the same set of circumstances as those under which he's previously run well (from a poor draw) and the chances are he'll do it again.

I could name literally dozens, although I'd then be labelled Mr Bore, not Mr Draw, but this is an approach that has kept me in profit every year since I can remember, and one I'd recommend anyone look into, if they haven't already done so.

It's not, though, an area that can be broken down statistically. Many have tried to work out draw biases by solely looking at past results and at where the horses that filled the first three places were berthed, but all have failed.

The problems here are manifold. Variables such as going, stalls position (high, centre, low), rails movements, watering, where the runners raced, whether they split into groups – all these things have to be taken into consideration.

_Simply looking at the bare result can't possibly achieve this.

No, the only way to keep on top of it all is to watch every sprint and keep a record. It's hard work, but it does pay off. I've been doing it for years, and it can become a chore during the summer, with no Sunday break for God knows how long, but I've yet to record a loss over a season.

I started writing a column in the *Racing & Football Outlook* last spring, and it's become a popular feature. If you don't buy the *Outlook* currently, I suggest you check it out, not because I write for it, but because it's a quality, well-produced paper.

There you'll find all the draw biases for the week to come, a list of horses who have run well from bad draws recently, and a look ahead to the coming week's action.

---

**CRAIG THAKE** *started* Racing Post's *'Ten Year Trends' column in the 1980s, kicking off with a notable success (described below). He tells us about his trends-based approach to finding winners.*

## Let History be Your Guide

FOR me, betting started at an early age when trips to the library resulted in me staying in the car while my father popped into the bookies. However, it wasn't long before I was handing him betting slips (he kept a multitude of them in the kitchen drawer) with 5p patents or 'ITV7's and investing my hard-earned pocket money.

Similarly, my father was a small-time punter never risking more than he could lose, but he did land the odd touch with a 10p Yankee full of outsiders and this usually coincided with my mum's birthday.

But by far the luckiest punter in the household was my younger sister. She only ever bet on the Grand National, but she had an uncanny habit of collecting winnings on a regular basis.

Her birthday fell on June the sixth, so her system revolved solely around backing the horse with racecard number six and her most lucrative moment came when Ben Nevis slogged around in the mud to win at odds of 40-1.

As a child, there seemed no logic to this system and I put it down to luck. However, in my teens I started to look into this phenomenon of why number six was so successful.

It soon came to light that it was a high-class handicap chaser, who was in the handicap proper, but who was not burdened with too much weight. My sister had unearthed a profitable system and anyone looking back at the National results during the 1980s and 1990s will find that most winners had saddle cloth numbers between four and ten.

If there was a historical angle to finding the winner of the National, then, logically, other races should follow suit. Even back in the 1980s, getting my hands on past results was not easy and it was not until I joined the *Racing Post* that I was able to study other races in detail.

In December 1986, I managed to persuade the editor to carry my historical analysis of the Welsh National. The selection, a progressive second-season chaser called Stearsby, duly obliged at odds of 8-1 and 'Ten Year Trends' was born – though many believe it should have been laid to rest there and then!

As I analysed more and more races, different historical factors came to the fore. Certain races favoured lightweights, others class horses, some were won by unexposed, progressive types and meetings like the Cheltenham Festival highlighted the importance of previous winning performances at Festivals gone by.

Perhaps the strongest historical factor that came to light was trainer trends, especially on the Flat, where trainers like Henry Cecil, Dick Hern, John Dunlop, Geoff Wragg and Michael Stoute all seemed to win the same races on a frequent basis.

Most punters pay little attention to historical factors. The exception is the draw – most know that it's folly to oppose the draw bias on certain courses, as it is in certain races, but better course management is reducing the draw's significance.

Most people assume the draw to be vital in sprints, but distance races like the Cesarewitch, Northumberland Plate and Ebor have a large draw bias.

However, the latter race does draw attention to problems in highlighting trends. So much has now been written about the low bias at York that, at the 2001 Ebor meeting, jockeys on the low-drawn horses all went off too fast and races were being won by high-drawn horses that were held up for a late effort.

I'll be the first to admit that punting solely around historical factors will not get you rich, but it is important to be aware of any historical biases.

In his days as 'Pricewise', Mel Collier had an enviable tipping record. He used many methods, but it was a rare event if he didn't ask me for a copy of my trends data first.

Historical factors may not always highlight the winner, but they will often steer you away from the bad value runners. For example, five-year-olds have dire records in the Champion and Stayers' Hurdles at the Cheltenham Festival, while horses out of the handicap rarely win the Grand National.

One question I have been asked more than any other is – why don't I cover more races? The answer's simple. I've found that the strongest trends exist in the most important races, as most of the field tend to be at their peak. Further down the scale, the fitness of a horse and a trainer's desire to win the race is less and so, understandably, fewer patterns emerge.

The worst type of race for historical analysis? Middle and low-grade sprint handicaps, mainly because there are too many of them and the outcome is determined by how the race is run.

Finally, should study be kept to ten years? Some might say no, because the more data you have the better, but others might say yes, because the further you go back the less relevant the racing is compared to now.

One thing's for sure – trends provide a useful edge in the never-ending war with the bookie fellows.

---

**PAUL JONES** *is author of the Cheltenham Festival Betting Guide, published by Weatherbys in updated form every March. He writes the 'Top Trends' column every week in* Raceform On Saturday.

## Once You Have Eliminated the Impossible . . .

IN betting, it often pays to begin by asking which horses are seriously up against it for a race, rather than rushing to embrace one that has an obvious chance.

I find that the more competitive the race, the harder it is to overcome strong negative trends and if, say, even only a quarter of the field can be ruled out with a degree of confidence by using history as a guide, then the betting percentages will have turned in the punter's favour.

If we can confidently rule out 50% of the book for any race, then, from a long-term profit perspective, we should be laughing. A large part of my betting strategy for the higher-profile races is to eliminate horses by using hard facts that have linked together losers in the past.

Very rarely will a horse with an extremely strong negative trend overcome history and the same can be said of runners that have more than one lesser negative trend to conquer.

I am a firm believer that analysing the whole result of a race rather than concentrating on what positive trends link together the winners will give a better overall picture of the type of horse that can be eliminated from further consideration for that race. For example, if the last ten winners of any given race carried less than 11st, then that is a strong statistic in its own right. But, if the placed horses have a similarly poor record to boot, then we really have something to go to war with (this is particularly true of the Grand National, of which more later).

Once I have my shortlist, only then will I take a view on the remaining runners by combining positive trends and all the usual factors that would go into the decision-making process. Although I would give greater respect to those horses that also fit the positive trends criteria, should they point to a horse that may have a problem with the race conditions (going, track or distance) it would be madness to keep blind faith and I would look elsewhere.

On the Flat, although there are a number of ways I eliminate runners, I find the most profitable to be via the draw in the major handicaps. In big-field events over a straight course, it is vital to be against horses drawn in the middle third.

Not only do such horses forfeit straight-line speed when tracking over to join one group or the other but, if they do decide to stay put and race down the middle, they are usually in a smaller group and find it hard to gain overall control of the race.

This is certainly true of the big five straight-course handicaps over a mile or less (Lincoln, Royal Hunt Cup, Wokingham, Stewards' Cup, Ayr Gold Cup). Over the last ten years, only six of the fifty renewals have been won by a runner drawn in the middle third of the field, at a strike rate of just 8.3%.

Clearly this falls way short of the usual probability laws, which suggest we should be hitting the target 33.3% of the time if we're selecting one third of the runners entirely at random.

For the big handicaps on round courses, we should not be putting too much faith in horses drawn on the outside. The John Smith's Cup at York is a perfect example. Incredibly, no winner has defied a double-figure draw in the last ten years. From a huge total of ninety-two to have attempted this feat, only five made the frame.

The principal reason for the collective failures of horses drawn on the outside is the often long, sweeping bend the field must take approaching halfway. Those drawn high can either race five deep, losing valuable lengths in the process, or drop in and pray the gaps appear at the right time, at a track where it's generally accepted that you should ideally race close to the pace.

Over the jumps, I find the strongest negative trend concerns horses saddled with big weights in staying events. History tells me that it is remarkably difficult to give weight away to rivals that are, more often than not, more likely to improve beyond their current handicap mark.

This is, of course, notwithstanding the fact that horses are far more likely to throw in the towel carrying a big weight over extreme distances and often in testing ground.

If we examine the results of the big five staying handicap chases in the last ten years (Hennessy Cognac Gold Cup, Welsh National, Grand National, Scottish National, Attheraces Gold Cup), on only five occasions has a horse successfully carried over eleven stones to victory.

The Grand National itself is a perfect example. As I write, eleven days before the 2002 renewal, we have to go back eighteen years to find the last horse to carry over eleven stones, while, in the last nine years, only two horses carrying a similar weight have even finished in the frame.

Given that continuity can be used by the punter as a valuable aid to finding winners and rooting out probable losers, in this new era of betting we should all be aware that there is more than one way to skin a cat. With spread betting (where we can bet horses to run badly) becoming more popular with each passing week, and the one-to-one betting exchanges giving we punters the opportunity to offer our own prices about runners we don't fancy, the sourcing of probable losers is at least as important as backing an outright winner.

With regards to a staking plan, unlike many punters, I try not to get suckered into the mindset that ties me down to one 'win single' bet per race. If I have two or three viable options left, having confidently eliminated most of the field, then I would divide my original stake and support the lot.

I've even been known to combine the shortlisted in Tote Exacta permutations, which I find can work extremely well when many of the field have been wiped out with a poor draw on the Flat.

On the other hand, if I found it hard to confidently rule out enough of the field, like in this year's Cheltenham Gold Cup, I would leave the race well alone. Just because it's a big race does not automatically mean a bet has to be struck.

Critics will argue that trends are there to be broken and, of course, at some point they inevitably will be. But what trends do is tell us what type of horse is required for specific tests and, as Nick Mordin once wrote: 'the higher up the class scale you go, the more rigid the requirements for winning such a race.'

Quite right.

---

*As a precocious teenager, **MARK HOWARD** wrote a book listing horses to follow for the coming jumps season, calling it* One Jump Ahead. *It was a hit and has been published annually ever since, expanding each year to include new features, while a companion for the Flat season,* Ahead On The Flat, *is also available every Spring.*

## Ferreting out the Best Prospects

I'M often asked for advice on how to produce successful books about horses to follow. My answer is usually the same; writing is relatively easy, publishing can be expensive and selling is the hard part.

So how did I succeed ? The answer is to produce a book which racing enthusiasts find informative and helpful, and offers value for money.

What should go into an annual 'horses to follow' book? Rather than pick the household names which the everyday punter recognises, I attempt to nominate horses which have yet to reach their full potential. But to do just that would not necessarily be enough to catch the eye of the ardent follower of National Hunt racing. Therefore, I always try to introduce new features and ideas into my publications.

In addition to selecting my top forty or fifty prospects, I consider how horses could be categorised. For example, many horses are purchased from the Flat to go jumping. I therefore have a regular section in *One Jump Ahead* called 'Changing Codes'. Irish point-to-point horses are another example and are listed under 'Pointers From Ireland'.

One can never be certain that such a method will appeal to all your readers but, provided those horses suggested win races, my customers are unlikely to object. After all, the best advertisement for any book of this kind is winners.

The emphasis of *One Jump Ahead* is on nominating horses which I consider have yet to reach their full potential. I place special emphasis on novices, both hurdlers and chasers; these I find the most exciting and, contrary to the belief of many, the most profitable in betting terms.

I must stress that, although I do have a bet, it is not my main concern and I do not consider myself a professional punter.

Before selecting horses for my book, I study, with other members of my family, hours of videos from the previous season. This is even more important when preparing to write my Flat book, *Ahead On The Flat*. It's very time-consuming but an invaluable and essential exercise. I also spend a lot of time studying the form book and back copies of the *Racing Post*. The internet has made life easier, in this respect.

I'm frequently asked if I follow any particular racing columnist. I have great respect for Gerald Delamere of the *Post* and I suppose I have probably been influenced by some of his thinking. I also read most of those who write in the *Daily Telegraph*, the *Post* and the *Racing Post Weekender*.

The stable interviews in my books are proving popular. When I first started writing at 17, I approached a number of the leading trainers (with some trepidation). On the whole, they have been very friendly and particularly helpful.

What they tell me is, on the whole, accurate and their information is invaluable, although, understandably, phrases such as 'well handicapped' are not what they like to read about their horses. Without the trainers, I would not be able to write my books to the level I would like and, for their help, I am very grateful.

There is one particular Newmarket trainer, whom I regularly visit for Ahead On The Flat. Each year, he has suggested I leave a certain horse out of the interview. Two years ago, one of those horses won three races that particular season and, last season, the nominated horse won seven races, including a Classic. It will be interesting to see if the trend continues.

As far as what I would term 'difficult' trainers are concerned, they are conspicuous by their absence in my publications. There are obviously those who are secretive, which, from an owner's point of view, I can appreciate.

I am fortunate to be able to do a job which brings me satisfaction and pleasure, most of the time. I can't claim to make a fortune but I do make a good living.

I try to put as much back into horse racing as I can, by regularly appearing on 'expert' panels for various Racing Clubs throughout the country, and support charities connected to the sport.

**KEN HUSSEY** *introduced his well-received speed-figures in the* Sporting Chronicle *in the early 1950s and soon did the business by tipping Pinza at 5-1 for the 1953 Derby. Spectacular coups landed in combination bets by fans of his speed figures have included wins of £93,000 and £44,000 in the 1970s and a £22,000 haul on the first day of the 1992 Cheltenham Festival. Ken provided the* Daily Star's *'Clockform' ratings for ten years before joining the* Racing & Football Outlook *in the early 1990s.*

## Lack of Information is Weighing Down Punters

AS reflected in race times, excessive weight can have a detrimental effect on speed, of that I have no doubts.

I am not talking here of a couple of pounds or so, but large lumps of surplus weight sometimes encasing the framework of our racing equine friends. There is a need, therefore, for weigh-bridges of industrial dimensions with which to appraise the bodyweights of runners on all racecourses, Flat and National Hunt.

Impassioned pleas for official on-course timepieces have been made by yours truly ever since the great Lester Piggott claimed 7lb, but the fragrant Jockey Club, and their front-men on the BHB, appear to be as deaf as a BOLA door-post when something likely to be of considerable benefit to betting shop dwellers and racegoers is proposed.

Yes, time stands still in more senses than one in British racing. Victorian grandstands, no grandstand (Bangor), primitive toilet facilities, third-world catering, paddyfield car parks . . . all overseen by racing's brown-hatted brigade.

As a result of official ineptitude, the form book can tell some very peculiar stories these days, and they don't make good, wholesome reading for cash-strapped punters regularly emptying wallets in the counting houses of those charitable chappies, the bookies.

One reason for those seemingly inexplicable defeats could be revealed through on-course scales big enough to stand the weight of our beloved four-legged friends.

Excess poundage should not be treated lightly. At the worst it can earn you a one-way ticket to the local crematorium for onward transmission to Heaven, Hades or Valhalla, depending on your religious persuasion.

From personal experience I can confirm that too much blubber in the carcass can drastically slow down the body's mainspring and final drive, reducing one's speed to that of an arthritic tortoise!

By now I trust that I have made it abundantly clear that a surfeit of weight, as confirmed by the clock, has a crippling effect on the speed of its unfortunate carrier.

There are certain time/speed practitioners who virtually regard weight as an insignificance. But, be that as it may, much concern is given by handicappers, trainers, owners and shrewd punters to the poundage a horse is to be burdened with in its attempt to be first to the winning post, and they cannot all be wrong surely?

The apparent lack of interest in electric race times on all tracks, as well as on-course weighbridges, shown by racing's blinkered authorities, is hard to comprehend.

Boxers are weighed. Greyhounds are life-long members of the official weight-watchers club. No dog dare don a racing jacket without a declaration of bodyweight being made public.

That certain successful racehorse trainers have their own weighbridges, as well as expert clock-holders, can be taken as irrefutable evidence that a set of heavy-duty scales, and reliable timepieces, can be worth their weight in winning betting slips.

These astute handlers know a horse's optimum body-weight by perusing previous evaluations, particular attention being paid to poundage (or Kilos) recorded on the day of the winning outing.

Variances of up to 20lb between appearances, and as much as 40lb or 50lb in the first few weeks of the campaign, are not, believe me, uncommon.

At present only those privy to the revelations of the stable's equine scales are able to judge whether or not a horse will be running at its most effective bodyweight.

Whilst race times are a vital necessity to evaluating form, it is also essential to know the disparity between a previous winning bodyweight and a current appraisal, an amount which could add up to the difference between success and failure.

So what, you may well ask, are the prospects of the nineteenth-century Racecourse Association rushing to install electric timing apparatus and weighbridges on all their tracks in time for the next millennium? At a guess, I would say that chances are as bright as England's brave cricket team beating the Aussies 5-0 in the next Test series, or Accrington Stanley winning the FA Cup!

*DAVE BELLINGHAM joined Raceform in 1997 as a horse-comment writer and became speed handicapper for the company in 2000. He writes a weekly column for the* Raceform Update *and* Raceform On Saturday, *as well as an All-Weather column for the* Racing & Football Outlook *during the Winter.*

## Why Crowbar Weight into Your Speed Figures?

I first dabbled in trying to compile my own speed ratings about ten years ago and I felt right from the start that this was the best way to measure a horse's ability.

After all, the fastest horse usually wins, so all I needed to do was to try and make my own system as accurate as possible. The only real problem I had was in trying to work out how much to adjust the raw speed figure for the weight differential.

Despite having tried a few combinations, I could never quite arrive at a value I was 100% happy with. So I took a random sample of a thousand horses and wrote a computer program to work out how much, on average, their speed ratings were affected by every 1lb more or less they carried than in their previous start.

When I ran the program, the results for those horses going up in weight were more or less what I had expected. For every 1lb more a horse carried, on average its speed figure was reduced by 0.4 of a point (on a scale of one point equalling 2.5 lbs).

All well and good so far, but for every 1lb less a horse carried, its speed rating also went down, this time by 0.3 of a point. I thought there must be a bug in my program or perhaps some faulty speed figures were distorting the results, but when I took a sample of a thousand different horses, the results were almost identical.

Closer inspection of a horse's profile showed that most who ran slower than in their previous start probably did so for reasons other than weight.

They may have been unsuited by the ground, the distance or the track. Perhaps they were lacking peak fitness or were drawn badly. None of these factors are reflected in conventional speed ratings.

In my opinion, weight-adjusted speed figures distort the true ability of a horse.

For example, if a Flat horse runs a raw, unadjusted speed figure of 56 while carrying 10st, and another horse runs an 84 carrying 8st, then adjusting to 9st will bring the two together at 70 (if 1lb equals one point on the scale).

If these two horses were then to meet at level weights, conventional speed figures would suggest that they had an equal chance, but in real life that just does not happen. The second of these horses has demonstrated the ability to run a good deal faster than the first and I would much rather make my own mind up about the effect of the revised weights than have the evidence tampered with before I was able to see it.

The idea that the horse with the bigger weight first time will somehow find the extra speed necessary to beat the other one simply because he has a stone less to carry today is fanciful, to say the least, especially in view of the results of my own research.

Taking this view has served me well in recent years, because it has revealed those horses that were genuinely faster than the opposition, as well as exposing those who can only run so fast, irrespective of the weight they carry.

A great example of the latter group is that professional loser Little John. He managed to finish second, third or fourth in each of his last sixteen outings in 2001 and earned consistent speed figures along the way, despite carrying as much as 10st10lb and as little as 7st5lb.

He would have been a tempting bet on more than one occasion using weight-adjusted figures, but viewing his ability in 'raw' terms showed him in a much truer light and certainly saved me a few quid.

---

**MARTEN JULIAN** *established one of the country's first independent racing advisory services in 1972 and was soon invited by* The Sunday Times *to create a column looking ahead to the week's races. 'Warm Up' quickly attracted a massive following, thanks to a steady stream of big-priced winners. Julian acquired a reputation as a specialist in unraced and less exposed horses and his first* Dark Horses *annual was written in 1976, since when he has produced and contributed to hundreds of publications.*

## Keen Observation Helps Evaluate the Mystery Horses

IT was after bowling my team captain out during a session in the nets that I first heard the term 'dark horse'.

'You're a bit of a dark horse,' my teacher remarked, as I turned to walk past him. Having enjoyed my first day's racing just a few days earlier, the remark seemed both well-timed and apposite. Some years later, when funds were needed to support my lifestyle as a third-year student, it occurred to me that there may be a few people willing to pay for my views on less-exposed, or even unraced, horses. Plenty was written then, as now, about top-class prospects from the leading yards, but there was nothing on the market which provided an informed view on the likely requirements or potential of lesser-known horses.

It was after thinking this through that I started to research for my first *Dark Horses* annual. I got Clement Freud to write the introduction (which he did for nothing), visited the local photocopying shop and had them bind the thing together.

That was in 1976. Now, almost three decades later, I'm still writing it every year, both for the Flat and the National Hunt. I'm pleased to say Clement (now Sir Clement) remains a friend and client.

Although it was generally thought that I had a network of well-placed contacts responsible for furnishing me with information, the truth is I very rarely spoke to anyone associated with a racing yard. I relied far more on a blend of intuition and careful scrutiny of the entries.

Many hours were spent delving into the entries that trainers had made for the big races, taking careful note of any unraced or lightly-raced maidens. This proved particularly useful with respect to the two-year-old races.

In those days it was much easier to try and gauge a trainer's thoughts because the entries, which were published in the Racing Calendar, had to be made three weeks in advance. Now we have five-day entries it seems remarkable that, in those days, trainers had to decide where to run their horses so far in advance. Yet, from my point of view, it proved enlightening. If, for example, a relatively little-known trainer had taken the trouble to enter a horse in a decent race, that was more than enough to point me in the right direction.

Sometimes, when speaking later with a trainer or contact, I was able to corroborate my thoughts.

I recall being one of the first people in the racing community to purchase a video recorder. It cost almost £800 and the tapes, which lasted only half an hour, were £15 each! However, it proved of immense value and probably gave me a significant edge over other race-readers. Don't forget that very little racing was televised. John Rickman, Lord Oaksey and the youthful Brough Scott occasionally covered midweek meetings, but generally only the major fixtures were seen on television.

This meant travelling many miles on poor roads. One year, during my days with the *Sunday Times*, I covered the best part of fifty thousand miles.

Yet hours spent studying yearlings at the sales, watching horses walk round the paddock before a race and talking with trainers and stable staff helped me learn how to detect the good from the bad. I began to appreciate a horse's eye and how it walked. I studied pedigrees and, after a few years, noted characteristics or traits that the horse had in common with its sire and dam.

A few golden rules? Pay great attention to detail and try, if possible, to go racing alone. Watch horses both at work and at play. Try to avoid backing maiden fillies. Never bet at Brighton or Bath. Keep a lookout for horses which possess a turn of foot. Try to detect a horse's attitude when it races.

Perhaps the best advice I've ever been given came from a battle-hardened Irish gambler. It went something like this:

'There was an old owl who sat in an oak. The more he saw, the less he spoke, The less he spoke, the more he heard. Why can't we all be like that wise old bird?'

Seems like good sense to me.

**JIM MCGRATH** *is best known as a commentator with Channel 4. He is also Managing Director of the Timeform Organisation.*

## Objectivity Helps Avoid the Punter's Pitfalls

AT Timeform, our editorial staff are trained to take an objective view of form. They are taught to analyse what has occurred in a race. Many punters lack objectivity because they home in on just one runner, almost inevitably the one they have backed!

Generally, it pays to concentrate on in-form and progressive horses, as opposed to those which may be well handicapped on efforts from the distant past. Of course, sometimes those in the last-named category pop up but, from a punting perspective, current form is usually the best guide.

All our staff have to pass a racing test and, apart from a general all-round knowledge of the sport, must show enthusiasm, a willingness to learn and come to the job with an open mind.

The worst habit many punters have is that they chase losses. If you are going to bet on a regular basis, you have to show discipline and accept that some days your homework won't work out.

The art of successful gambling is to cut down or eliminate losers. Most of us, from time to time, find a few winners. By being selective or, if you like, staying out when a race looks tough, you'll improve your strike-rate and, thus, your overall profit.

Sticking to the better quality races generally gives you a stronger chance of success. Quite often the midweek racing programme is lacking in that respect but, at the weekend, there are usually a handful of decent contests to have a crack at. Whilst the betting-shop punter has a chance of making it pay, I believe it's an advantage to go racing regularly. Especially when assessing maiden races, paddock inspection is vital. Being track-side gives one the edge over those punting from the shop.

Value is a very important betting concept. It's also quite straightforward; a horse is a value bet if, in your opinion, it is on offer at a price bigger than you estimate its chances. Look to increase your stakes when you are winning and to cut back when you hit a dodgy spell. Allocating oneself a specific betting bank helps to induce the discipline needed to do this properly.

Given an understanding of value, plus a strike-rate of one winner in every three or four bets, you should do alright in the main. Confidence, or lack of it, affects one's prospects of success; you must have faith in your own judgement, particularly when things go wrong.

Many years ago I met Geoffrey Boycott in a TV studio, who explained the theory he took with him every time he went into bat. His approach resonated with mine towards punting. Boycott used to get particularly annoyed with young batsman who returned to the pavilion after failing, moaning about when they would next get fifty or a century.

Geoff always went out with the aim of scoring one, then two, and so on. The moral to punters is don't go for big hits straightaway; build your confidence with a few successful small bets first. In other words, take things stage by stage.

# CHAPTER 11
# BETTING AT SHORT PRICES

TO put it bluntly, supporting short-priced favourites in single bets on a regular basis is inadvisable for all but the consummate professional. Even without tax, the average punter should regard backing anything at 2-1 or less as an expensive luxury.

From time immemorial, bookmakers' satchels have been filled by those prepared to back favourites indiscriminately and their romance with such punters can blossom into a full-blown affair when the poor gambler doubles up in an attempt to get out of trouble.

Fortunately, playing at short odds is anathema to most punters. Unless you're a particularly disciplined and knowledgeable player, it's both cheaper and more fun to back those at bigger prices, adhering to that wise old saying 'odds-on, look on.'

Flexibility and the ability to change your tactics are imperative in order to stay solvent. Try to become a player of extremes, aiming to build up a small bank via your safety shots, then use that profit to subsidise more expensive, potentially much more profitable bets, like a Placepot.

With so much racing going on, I find it easier these days to link up two to four horses with approximate odds of between 1-2 and 2-1 in doubles, trebles or a four-timer, than to find one winner that might show a similar return for a win single.

Following my multiple-bet method becomes simpler in the summer, on Saturdays, Bank Holidays and when there's evening racing. At such times there's more racing, offering more choice and I find that Sundays especially feature many hot favourites at value prices.

Win singles at less than 2-1 are of little help to most punters, offering very little in the way of a margin for error. Use such bets as bankers, if you feel especially confident about their chances, but mostly for coupling with other short-priced shots and for pool betting.

## Guide to short-price doubles and trebles

*Two winners at Evens = 3-1 double*
*Three winners at Evens = 7-1 treble*
*Two winners at 6-4 = 5.3-1 double*
*Three winners at 6-4 = 14.6-1 treble*
*Two winners at 2-1 = 8-1 double*
*Three winners at 2-1 = 26-1 treble*

## Finding a banker

On the Flat, three-year-old maidens from May onwards can prove profitable, as can juvenile maiden and conditions races from mid-May. Beware of any ground changes and don't play if the ground is soft or worse. From the second week in September, results swing in favour of the bookmakers unless there's a continuing and prolonged spell of dry weather.

Over the jumps, stick to novice hurdles and juvenile hurdles, where experience is at a premium and those runners who've already made a good impression are very likely to go well again.

Note, however, that bad midwinter ground will make upsets likely.

Summer jumps racing often provides prime banker material, thanks to novice hurdlers trained by Messrs Pipe or Hobbs, with McCoy or Johnson their 'angels on horseback', providing manna from heaven for the beleaguered punter.

Whatever the race, a banker should have the following pre-requisites; suitable ground, a good draw where applicable, a leading trainer and jockey in form, and a suitable course and distance.

It should be the clear best on form. It should not be up against an unraced or unexposed type from a top stable, which would undermine my confidence, if not yours. Fear the unknown.

Hurdlers must have shown fluency in previous starts and suffer no stamina problems. Hard-pullers must never be regarded as banker material under any code.

Having reached your own opinion, you can confirm it or get a professional lead on such races by checking the 'training centre' section of the *Racing Post*. This provides unparalleled information, both positive and negative. If it should align with your own judgement, then what you have is dynamite with the fuse lit.

Keep in mind that raising your normal stakes to support a short-priced favourite or that 'good thing' you've been given is courting disaster. Instead, aim to get a lot from a little, from speculative bets subsidised via canny punting, through coupling and so on, in the manner suggested or in a way which suits your betting stratagem.

## Try a chart forecast . . .

The chart forecast offers the shop punter a chance to support short-priced horses when circumstances appear favourable and you can take advantage of the available prices, which fluctuate with rapidity. It's better value than the SP alternative, where it is odds-on that one or both of the first two horses home will have been on offer at longer odds than their SP.

The serious backer concentrates on a race with a good thing and, for him, only one conceivable second choice – the betting could be 1-2, 5-2, 14-1 bar. There are many such races on Sundays in the summer, when appearance money encourages trainers to run their no-hopers, whose owners get a day out in the happy knowledge that the industry is helping to cover their costs.

Here you have to be equally sure that your second-favourite is as certain to thrash the remainder as it is certain to be runner-up to the market leader.

This is not a bet to take lightly – remember, you are laying odds-on twice to get a minimal return – but, on occasions, it does represent a minor bank raid.

A word of warning, however – I repeat, don't play if there are unraced or unknown quantities among the opposition, especially if they're from leading yards. They may appear unfit or unfancied but, with class and scope on their side, can run on and upset calculations.

Avoiding handicaps and steeplechases with this bet is an obvious precaution.

The chart forecast can be usefully employed in many other ways, too – for example, when you expect the hot favourite to be beaten by the second or third-favourite. The betting could be 4-5, 7-2, 9-2, 12-1 bar and you fancy the 9-2 shot, making the 4-5 your only danger. You can stake two points on the 9-2 shot to win, with the favourite second, and cover it with the favourite to win and your selection second.

At the other end of the scale, a small field of five to seven runners with a wide-open betting market (i.e. 10-3, 7-2, 9-2, 5-1 and so on) will offer 12-1 the field in the forecast market and you can take three against the rest, incorporating six straight forecasts, and you'll know your return in advance if any should be successful. What you see is what you get and it is a bet to keep on your side for when the occasion arises.

The value here lies in the prices on offer early on, not in the returned SP forecast dividend. If you are quick, can calculate percentages and define a two-horse race at source, you can certainly benefit from snapping up the odds on offer. These change with the odds currently offered on each horse. Never accept SP forecast returns when you can take a forecast price.

If you are playing with first and second-favourites, you can be reasonably certain of beating the SP return. Even if the hot favourite is not shortened for SP, the next best is likely to be cut and, unlike 'win' betting (where the second or third show can be best), if you are satisfied that the front two are alone against the rest, then take the first chart price on offer.

You can cover a three-point forecast with a point on the reverse forecast, or with a point forecast on your first choice to win and your third pick to be second.

## . . . or an Exacta!

The Tote threw down the gauntlet to the SP forecast by replacing its Dual Forecast bet with the Exacta, which, just like the forecast, requires punters to nominate the first two home in the right order.

The value, as with all bets, lies in knowing when to play and, when doing so, whether the Exacta or the forecast is your best bet.

Since its inception, the Exacta has proved that it offers distinct advantages over its predecessor.

With the Dual Forecast, punters nominated two horses and got paid if they were first and second, regardless of the order. If the first two home were the odds-on favourite and the 33-1 outsider – the Dual Forecast paid exactly the same whether the outsider was first and the favourite second or if they finished the other way round.

That might suit you if you'd been sure that the favourite would win – you'd get paid even if the shock result occurred. But if you'd fancied the outsider to win, you'd feel aggrieved at having to share the fruits of your perspicacity with many others who'd had less imagination.

Now, with the Exacta, punters have a much greater degree of control and can juggle their stakes and preferences to suit themselves. Alongside the forecast, punters enjoy a real choice, which was more of a Hobson's choice in the days of the Dual Forecast.

Tote dividends are declared to a £1 unit but your basic stake can be less, so long as the total perm adds up to £1 or more.

If you fancy two horses equally, you can do a simple reverse Exacta (those two to be first and second in either order) which will cost you twice your stake. On most occasions, this may not be the case – happily, with the Exacta, your options are legion.

Let's say your fancies are 6-4 and 7-2 and you expect them to finish in that order. Split your stake (we'll say it's £5) as follows;

a) £3 forecast, the 6-4 shot to beat the 7-2 shot and

b) £1 reverse exacta

If the clear favourite wins, the forecast will generally pay more than the Exacta. If it doesn't, or if the 7-2 shot wins with the favourite second, the Exacta element will probably provide ideal compensation, returning your stake with a profit.

Reversing the cover is something most punters tend not to think of unless they're perming three or four from a large field. If you fancy the favourite and are looking to place a number of forecasts or Exactas in which the favourite is nominated to beat two or three others, consider giving yourself the reverse cover as well. After all, the dividend will be significantly higher if the favourite is beaten.

As with all Tote pool betting, a disproportionate amount of stakes will be placed on the leading jockeys, on trainers in form or on any horse which gets a lot of press coverage. If you want to include such popular fancies in a bet like this, favour the forecast over the Exacta. On the other hand, if you're going against the crowd, go for the Tote bet.

Bear in mind that horses who start as favourites but drift in the market to a bigger price will increase the dividends of those betting on the forecast, while the Exacta dividend is unlikely to be improved.

Exacta betting can be especially profitable on Saturdays, Sundays, Bank Holidays and at evening meetings. On such occasions, there's a high proportion of 'holiday' money going into the Tote pools at the track and such money tends to be spread around fairly evenly.

The bookies might be betting 7-4, 2-1 and 8-1 bar two, but, if the front two in the betting romp home to fill the first two places, the Exacta sometimes pays surprisingly well at such meetings, thanks to the optimism of the amateur punters who backed the long-shots.

High-staking punters should note, however, that the Exacta can suffer from weak pools away from the major meetings. In such cases, they may find that they're basically betting against themselves and that their own stake money forms most of the pool. For such high rollers, the advice must be – stick to the forecast.

# CHAPTER 12
# THE PROS

From a lowly position as a sub with Raceform, **HENRY RIX** has risen to become one of the UK's most expensive private tipsters, via successful stints with the Today newspaper and the Racing Post. Recently, he's also enjoyed success as an owner, his best horse being Stewards' Cup winner Tayseer.

## Do Your Homework and You Have a Chance

I don't go racing. I know some gamblers prefer to, so they can have a look at the horses in the paddock and so on, but I'd have no idea what to look for in a racehorse.

I might just about be able to tell if it were fit, but I reckon I'd be put off more often than encouraged. What could be worse than fooling yourself that you're a paddock judge and putting yourself off a 33-1 winner?

My approach is purely analytical. I have stacks of theories and use them to develop my own approach to finding winners.

I keep an eye on various ratings of all kinds, including speed ratings. I reckon you could do well just by following a reliable set of ratings, but it's common practice for many people to do that now and that means it's harder to get a value price. I know of a particular set of ratings in America that became so popular, their top-rated was basically guaranteed to be favourite.

To be successful, you have to be one step ahead of everyone else, but there are definitely more people these days who know what they're doing when they're betting on horses.

One thing I've been working on is a theory that people don't really understand racehorse pedigrees in this country, outside the breeding industry. It's an underused factor in betting. I think there's some mileage to be got out of assessing the going preferences of a horse's ancestors and whether they acted round certain tracks.

The problem for most punters is that they just don't know enough. Mostly, they won't have put in anything like as much work as I do when I'm studying a race.

Having got the declarations at 1pm the day before, I'll be working on the next day's racing until 7pm or later and then again the next morning. It's the big handicaps that I love, especially on the Flat. I'll look at them from the five-day stage and it wouldn't be uncommon for me to put in ten hours on a race like the Wokingham.

It's the puzzle of it that attracts me to these races, their complexity. Because they're harder, fewer people will do enough work to pick out the good bets, so it should be easier to get a decent price.

I also like betting on races at the top tracks. For a lot of those races, people get preconceived ideas about which horse will be best, especially when the media go over the top about a horse that might turn out to be good.

I don't miss betting in the ring, charging around looking for the best price and then getting knocked back when you try to have a bet – it drove me mad.

Internet betting exchanges are the way forward. You can bet anonymously on markets of increasing strength. On the first day of the 2002 Cheltenham Festival, I saw a bet of £50,000 on Like-A-Butterfly being matched on one of the sites and that will become the common practice.

For a minor race meeting in midweek, there can be a lot more wagered over these sites than in the ring, so you don't have to be a great tipster to see where the future of betting lies.

---

**ALAN POTTS** had his first bet at the age of 13 – he was paid out, too, but wasn't hooked until he had his first glimpse of live racing, while playing in a schoolboys' cricket match; the pitch was set in the middle of the loop at Alexandra Park racecourse. Since he was made redundant from his job as a computer consultant in 1991, Alan has made his living as a professional gambler.

## Always Challenge the Accepted Wisdom

I'VE written two books covering how I go about betting on horseracing, so it's hard to give a brief insight into what I regard as the best way to go about it, but I think the basic point is that every punter should have some kind of strategy.

Some of the advice I gave in my books is already out of date, but my aim with both was to get people thinking about their gambling. It's amazing how few people do this, but gambling is like any other field of endeavour – if you don't have a plan or an objective in mind, then you've got very little chance of achieving anything.

Betting is one of two things in life that everyone thinks they can do well without any training – and I've learned (from women) that most men are rubbish at both!

You also have to be able to modify your approach as times change. In the 1970s, it was possible to make good money if you knew which horses acted on soft ground, and in the 1980s if you were aware of the draw bias at a particular course – hardly anyone else knew the importance of such things.

These days, that kind of information is readily available in the racing media, so you have to be constantly adjusting your strategy in order to stay ahead. For that reason, I spend more time on research, far more than I spend poring over the formbook.

Research into new ideas is more likely to make you money in the long term than reminding yourself of what individual horses have achieved in the past.

For example, I've been having a look at David Loder's record with two-year-olds in pattern races during the 2001 season. Most people will think he did well in such races, because the hype has all been about how good he is with juveniles, but the truth is he did poorly. I found twelve examples of him having the beaten favourite in such races, against only three winners.

However, because of the general perception that his two-year-olds are unbeatable, his charges are over-backed, meaning that there ought to be some value in those races for anyone prepared to oppose them.

If I could offer one piece of advice to punters generally, it would be that they should specialise. There's so much racing nowadays that you can't possibly hope to keep up with all the form lines and everything that's happening.

I concentrate on good-class racing. I think it's generally true to say that the better the race, the better the bet. On the Flat, I normally restrict myself to eight of the top courses and I'd rarely bet in any race worse than a 0-85 handicap.

It's also true that the lower the grade of a race, the less consistent are the horses contesting it. They generally have a quirk or two, whether it's a physical problem or a mental issue that makes them unappealing for betting purposes, even in a race that might suit them ideally.

I part-own a few moderate horses that run at the lower levels of the game, so I'm familiar with the nature of the beast. And because the handicap mark is so important to such horses, there's always the temptation to run them down the field to gain a few pounds' advantage for the future. That can be done without breaking any rules, just by running over the wrong trip, or on unsuitable going. For many punters, spotting these sorts of moves is part of the fun, but as I'm making my living, I'd rather be betting at Ascot or York than Folkestone or Catterick.

I'd say that, at the lower levels, jump racing is probably more straightforward than Flat racing but it's harder to make money – principally because of the number of professional punters you typically find at the jumps. Even on a wet Monday at Fontwell, you'll see twelve to fifteen full-time players in the ring and maybe half of the money taken will be theirs.

There are fewer at most Flat meetings, where you're also betting against more mug money. When I'm racing at Goodwood in the summer, there'll be maybe fifty coaches in the car park, all having brought recreational gamblers to the track. At Fontwell, you'd be lucky to see one.

I don't rely on ratings of any kind, I don't see the point. Most ratings are weight-adjusted in some way and, for me, weight just isn't that important. I concentrate more on the shape of a race, which horses are suited by the trip, the track, the going, what the pace will be like, what's the draw bias and so on.

I'd say eighty per cent of turf races aren't truly-run, in the sense of having an end-to-end gallop, so you couldn't rely on speed ratings to give you a clear picture about those races. Just because a horse wins in a slow time doesn't mean that he can't run faster if necessary.

I won't spend hours with the form book, but will instead rely on my memory of what I've seen these horses do before. For example, I remember recently backing a horse that had previously run very well in the face of a draw bias that should have counted strongly against it.

Next time, it was in a field of twelve, of whom six had never won a handicap and four others had never won over the trip or on a straight track. I reckoned I was backing one of only two with a realistic winning chance. The horse obliged at 7-2 from early 9-2.

There's nothing very difficult about any of this, but most people just don't look at things in that way.

If you try to make it as a full-time gambler, you'll have to be able to cope with losing runs. This is what knocks out most punters, who just can't handle the bad times, whether psychologically or because they don't start with a big enough bank.

To succeed, you must not be easily swayed by the opinions of others. You have to work out your own ideas and stand by them. I don't think it's a coincidence that so many pro punters come from analytical/logical backgrounds; many had previous careers connected with computers, statistics, maths, the City and so on.

If you're a more emotional type, if you feel like jumping up and down every time you get a winner, you'll struggle to get through the losing periods.

As Kipling said, you have to be able to treat triumph and disaster just the same.

*Having started work with the* Racing & Football Outlook *in the mid-1980s, EDDIE FREMANTLE moved to the* Sporting Life *for four years before leaving in 1993 to become a full-time professional gambler. Nicknamed 'Eddie the Shoe', he made his living backing horses for eight years but has recently fallen back into journalism as* The Observer's *main racing correspondent.*

## Hold Your Nerve and Accept the Inevitable Losers

THERE'S no substitute for doing your homework. When I'm going racing, I look at every horse in every race on the card, trying to consider every angle.

It means that I spend a lot of time with the form book and I dabble with various ratings. I follow some speed figures and I keep my own ratings for juvenile handicappers. I did try to maintain my own handicap for all racehorses but it's such a gargantuan effort that I gave it up fairly quickly.

I know some people say you should specialise and stick to one particular kind of race but I've never agreed with that. You should bet on any race in which you can win. Having said that, I tend to avoid the top-class meetings, because the form is so public that you can't get an edge. I'd sooner bet in the lower grades, where you've got a chance of finding out something that most people don't know.

My fellow contributor Alan Potts once wrote a book about betting called 'Against The Crowd' and I believe that's the best philosophy for any punter – do something different. If you follow the same pattern as everyone else, you're very unlikely to succeed. Looking for value is certainly important, though a lot of rubbish is talked about value. I'm more interested in anti-value, finding favourites at artificially short prices and taking them on. I'll back two or more to beat a false 'fav' and sometimes I'll fall on the winner.

You have to take a long-term view and have faith in your judgement. Everyone gets losing runs, so things will go wrong at some point, but you have to try and keep doing what you've been doing and, if your judgement's good, you'll be alright in the long run.

I've been betting on horses for eight or nine years, consistently doing OK and, when I get a bad run, it helps to remember that. The psychological side of gambling is massive and I've struggled with this in the past, but the best punters I know don't worry about losing; they have an arrogance that helps them keep going.

There are two especially big gamblers that I often see at the track, one a bookmaker, the other a gambler. They'll bet each other at anything, the flip of a coin, or whether most winners on a day's racing will have odd saddlecloth numbers or even. They'll regularly bet each other hundreds of pounds on such things and win or lose without caring.

I think you're a long way towards being a successful gambler if you can treat money in such a lackadaisical way. It means your judgement isn't distorted by psychological factors, like fear or the need to win. For these guys, betting in big sums on trivia is just a way of livening up a dull afternoon and, because they're usually betting on 50/50 outcomes, they know they'll be about even in the long run.

Of course, there's more information available nowadays and some people say that means we're better punters, but you have to be aware that the information's available to bookies and other punters as well. It just means that, to get an edge, you have to be a lot better than you used to have to be.

I remember in the late 1980s I used to go to the point-to-points in East Anglia and found that I would then know more about the form for hunter chases under Rules than anyone else, including the bookies. One day at Fakenham, I was looking to oppose a weak favourite in a hunter and realised I'd recently seen the fourth-favourite beat one of those ahead of it in the market in a point-to-point, as well as another that was on offer at about the same price.

I backed it and it won, which I suppose is why I remember the story, but that sort of thing just doesn't happen now – the papers can tell you all about the 'points' form and everyone knows.

Another piece of common wisdom that I disagree with is this idea that you shouldn't chase your losses. For me, it's more important to chase than not to bet.

Some people, having backed a winner or two early on in a day's racing, will then stop, even if they've studied the whole card and come to the track prepared to bet in each race. But then, the next time they go racing, they're betting again, so it's not as if they've given up for good. So why stop just because you're up on the day?

If you're losing and you don't chase, then you'll never get out of trouble. A punter who can't have a bet is like a golfer with the yips or a darts player who can't let go of the dart. It's the worst way to be.

Punters should try to keep their turnover high and bet as often as possible. It keeps you in the game and takes the pressure off. If you only bet rarely, but have a big bet when you do, you really have to get it right.

For me, it makes more sense to divide that one stake up and have fifty bets in the same time, at a fiftieth of the stake. You'll get more winners, the losers will matter less and your confidence will go up.

Personally, I prefer going to the track to bet, I need to see the racing in three dimensions. Television never shows the whole way the race pans out and you can always watch a replay afterwards; seeing the race from the track gives you a fresh angle on what happens that no-one else gets.

*Having won the* Racing Post's *Naps table for* Raceform On Saturday, **MARK NELSON** *enjoyed a successful stint with the* Racing & Football Outlook *before joining* The Sun.

## Search for the Logic Behind Each Winner

LOOKING back, it's easy to determine when my betting took a turn for the better.

It came about after an innocent question by a friend many years ago. It should be remembered that at the time we were all very much novices, spending more time looking at the bottom of our pint pots than at the backsides of horses.

I was racing one day at Goodwood with a few friends and, as normal, we struggled in the handicaps, where the lure of fancy prices enticed us to part with most of our money. This led to the crucial question from one of our party, who asked 'how come that beast won today, but hasn't managed to get anywhere close on his last few outings?'

It was a good question, one that got me thinking. If we knew exactly why a horse had won, then we would have an idea of whether it was likely to reproduce that level of form again.

Plenty of research followed. The scrutiny of past results only went to show that many winners failed to win again on their next start. These were generally the handicappers that had been about for many seasons and whose level of ability had already been established.

If they dropped to a suitable handicap mark, you could expect them to pick up a race but, as soon as the handicapper had reassessed them, it was unlikely they would win again for a while.

The horses we wanted to support were those that could be confidently expected to follow up a recent win. It became clear that many of these types had a definite reason for winning. Gelding appeared to be a big issue, as, once a horse had been cut, it was not unusual to see a significant upturn in its form.

Several other reasons became apparent too. A change of trainer sometimes made an impact, as did a change of running style (from making the running to being held-up), a different track type (turning or straight) and young, lightly-raced horses seemed to improve naturally.

As a young man, fairly new to betting, I appeared to have found the key. If a horse had shown improvement to win a race and there was clear reasoning as to why, then surely they could be supported to do so again, granted similar conditions.

What seemed to be the most significant point about this 'discovery' was that, prior to the improvement, the horse in question would most likely have shown relatively poor form. This would mean that the animal would be reasonably well treated at the start of its winning sequence and, as such, should have the ability to win a few more times before the handicapper had its measure again.

It all seems so obvious now and plenty of punters are using similar techniques every day. But, as a spotty adolescent all those years ago, it was as if I was the only person to have made a breakthrough and it felt great.

At the time, I was between jobs and had taken some part-time work as an office cleaner. It was a fancy hi-tech office building, where the only work required was to answer my pager and attend whatever floor needed assistance.

It usually involved emptying waste paper bins, shredders and the like. Not the most glamorous of jobs and certainly not the most taxing. But, importantly, it meant that, between these 'office emergencies', I could bury myself in the day's *Racing Post* and try to establish why horses had won the previous day.

After this, I would scan the entries for the week ahead and it was a great feeling when everything dropped into place. The adrenalin really started flowing when the clock neared my 2.00pm knock-off time, when I would walk down the local bookies on my way home to stick a few quid on, and watch the day's racing.

At the time, my job situation may not have looked too good to the casual observer, but it allowed me the time to immerse myself in what was to become a real passion. The suits in the big office may not have spared a second thought for the short-haired fellow emptying their bins, but nothing could take away the feeling of having backed the winner of the 2.30 and I knew there would be plenty more to come.

# CHAPTER 13
# GAMBLERS' TALES

*JOHN OAKSEY was champion amateur rider over the jumps in 1958 and 1971, winning the Whitbread and Hennessy Gold Cups on his beloved Taxidermist. He has since pursued successful careers as broadcaster, journalist and after-dinner speaker. Thanks to Channel 4 colleague John McCririck, he is known to millions as 'The Noble Lord'.*

## Making the Most of Mixed Fortune

I never had much luck punting, even in the days when I was usually riding as well. I remember a mare called Cautious that I owned with a few others and rode in her races, towards the end of the 1950s. We all thought she was a knock-down certainty for a novice hurdle and we backed her heavily twice in a row, but she ran appallingly badly on both occasions.

We concluded that she wasn't as good as we thought. Next time Cautious ran, at Wincanton, she was completely unfancied and we certainly didn't have a penny on. The ground, however, was fast and this was the first time that she'd run on such going – it turned out to be exactly what she wanted!

As we raced up with the pace, it became clear to me that we had every chance of winning and I panicked. At this time, I had only ridden a couple of winners and I certainly had no idea how to lose a race. Cautious was absolutely running away with me but, by managing to steer rather wide round the bends, I managed to finish no better than fourth.

My mother met me afterwards and said how wonderful it was that we'd done so well. Unfortunately, she'd forgotten her binoculars and hadn't been able to see the race.

'But don't worry,' she said, 'General McCreery was nearby, so I got him to watch it for me and tell me what you were doing.' I may have paled a little at this news, for

General McCreery was senior steward at the time, but all he said to me was 'That ran well, John.'

I'm happy to say that Cautious and I got it right next time, at Chepstow, when the money was down and my friends got paid at 6-1.

At about this time, I started writing previews of races for *The Daily Telegraph* under the pen name of 'Marlborough'. I wrote a long preview for the second running of the Whitbread and ended with something like 'If any miracles do happen, then I suppose Taxidermist might win.'

It was what you might call inside information, as I was due to ride 'Taxi', but unfortunately my article was slightly over-long and the sub-editor cut out the tip. It was a shame, because Taxi and I won well, at odds of 100-6 (a shade over 16-1).

Afterwards, I congratulated the winning trainer Fulke Walwyn, who also trained the runner-up, Mandarin. 'It must have been great,' I said, 'to see your horses sail over the last together like that.'

'Great?' he yelled. 'It was a disaster! I had my boots on Mandarin.' I hadn't known that before the race, not that I'd have done a thing differently if I had known.

It just goes to show that your information can be as inside as you please, but horseracing remains a highly unpredictable business.

I eventually gave up gambling altogether. I found that I was losing more or less consistently and, with uncharacteristic self-control, I decided to stop.

I went out with a winner, though.

Working for Channel 4, I was helping to prepare for their coverage of the 1993 running of the 2,000 Guineas. Graham Goode and I were recording voice-overs for one of the French two-year-old races from the previous season, won very impressively by a horse of Andre Fabre's.

This horse, Zafonic, did something I've never seen before or since. He came into shot so suddenly and travelling so quickly that he beat the cameraman, running across the screen and out of shot before the camera caught up again.

John McCririck had seen him win that day and was impressed. Graham and I had our maximum bets on Zafonic, who won quite emphatically on the day.

If only all my fancies did that well. I remember getting a letter from a disgruntled viewer, sent to me through Channel 4. 'Dear Bastard,' it said, 'you couldn't tip more rubbish if they bought you a fork-lift truck.'

The truth is, the only way to make money from betting on horses is pure hard work. I haven't managed it, but I know people who have and I'd say the best judge among them is Jim McGrath, who now heads Timeform.

To get it right, you need to combine serious form study with a determination to go racing as often as possible. I believe Jim would have been at the races most days of his life.

It's vital that you know what a horse is supposed to look like when it's fit but, as my own experience shows, even if you can do that, it's not an easy game!

*A veteran columnist with the* Sporting Life, **DAVID ASHFORTH** *writes a thought-provoking Saturday column for the* Racing Post. *He is a long-suffering punter and the record of his misfortunes is recorded in his gambler's autobiography,* Hitting The Turf.

## Luck

THE Lord works in mysterious ways but, in my experience, all of them end up with you getting stuffed.

It's difficult to believe in a benevolent supreme being when the horse you have backed has just collapsed in an inelegant heap after jumping the last.

It wouldn't be quite as bad if it had been the first fence but, no, it has to be the last, when 20 lengths clear. That's the way it works. Luckily, I can help.

Over 30 years of punting have taught me three important lessons. One, don't make the mistake of thinking that some outcomes just aren't possible. They are. Two, however much you think you could lose in one day's spread betting, it's actually a lot more. Three, it's best to stop before you have to sell your house.

It's a long time since I had a house but, once, I had an extraordinary stroke of good fortune. It was at Huntingdon, on 20th May 1972. I had backed a horse owned by Paul Mellon, trained by Bob Turnell, ridden by Bill Rees, and named Hay Field. It was a two-mile novices' chase.

As Hay Field approached the final fence, there were two things standing between him and victory, not counting the fence. The first was Retrospect, ridden by Philip Blacker, and the second was Essira, ridden by Andy Turnell.

Both were in front of Hay Field, both were going better than Hay Field and, barring accidents, both were going to finish in front of Hay Field.

Retrospect fell, Essira was brought down, and Hay Field was left to win. I know you should never want a horse to fall (a few blunders are quite acceptable) but my joy was matched only by Woodland Poacher's easy success at 10-1 in the next.

I cling to this memory like a shipwreck victim to flotsam, or it might be jetsam. Every time misfortune strikes, I tell myself, 'but remember Hay Field,' and I do.

The trouble is, I also remember Auriol Sinclair, and John Bosley, and a host of others. Mrs Sinclair's Simian was clear at the last at Ascot, on 22nd November 1969, at 13-2, but wasn't clear shortly afterwards, having forgotten to clear the last. Fada cleared the last at Fontwell on 29th December 1986, at 20-1, but something unfortunate had befallen me in a telephone kiosk a little earlier.

I was standing in the kiosk, about to say, 'Twenty pounds each-way Fada, please,' when the door opened. I recognised the intruder immediately. It was my wife.

There are times in life when 'Twenty pounds each-way Fada, please,' doesn't seem the right thing to say. This was one of them, so I didn't say it. For a while, I didn't say anything. Eventually, my wife broke the silence. 'What are you doing?' she asked.

It was a reasonable question and I searched hard for a reasonable answer. I couldn't find one, so I waited for a coronary, in the hope that she would feel sorry for me. While I waited, Fada was winning by 30 lengths. Thank you, God.

Once, I grew a string of photo-finish defeats that was so long I didn't dare mention it, knowing that no-one would believe me. I wasn't sure I believed it myself but, eventually, as the string grew longer and longer, it developed a curious fascination. There was a certain comfort in the increasing certainty that, if it was a photo-finish, I had lost. You probably know the feeling.

Eventually, I might have followed the example of a punter in a betting shop in Bradford, who reached such a state of despair that he used to stand in the middle of the shop, waving his betting slip in the air and shouting, 'See this. This is a tenner on the next favourite – and this is what it's worth.'

Then he tore up the slip and threw the pieces in the air. 'Help yourself, maties, because they aren't worth a thing.' And he was right, they weren't.

When my string of photo-finish defeats finally ended, one day at Epsom in 1979, it was slightly disturbing, as if even that small certainty in life had been destroyed.

Luckily, I was only seven when Devon Loch made himself famous in 1956 but, at a humbler level, like all of us, I have my own special memories. There was the day when I backed Harbour Bazaar, and his jockey forgot to weigh in, and the day I sold SPs at Fontwell, then watched as Master Comedy won at 33-1, Woodlands Boy at 50-1, and Polish Rider, also at 50-1.

In the old days, when someone committed suicide, the coroner invariably recorded that the victim took his own life while the balance of his mind was disturbed. Hardly fair on spread bettors.

On the other hand, remember Hay Field.

*Sports journalist* **LAURA THOMPSON** *has written about the attractions of racing and gambling for the* Racing Post, The Guardian *and* The Observer. *She is the author of two books about the sport:* Newmarket *and* Quest For Greatness.

# The System

SUMMER 2000 – and the year when I thought I had cracked gambling forever. The year when I won money and honestly believed that I would always do so. When I planned to write a book about how I had done it, and make even more money to add to what I could not stop winning. When I had a system, a gorgeous working system all of my own: Thrown In Theory (T.I.T.).

I had never been much for systems, not until then. Either there is something stubbornly mad about them, or else they're exhaustingly scientific and require hours of study, as if you were sitting a maths 'A' level every morning of your life. Gambling on horses has always seemed to me to hover somewhere between madness and science. Surely that's the fun of it?

So my system was something else altogether: a lazy system for a lazy gambler, an intuitive system for an intuitive gambler. It came to me in a sunlit flash of loveliness as I was going through the *Racing Post* one morning, and my eyes sizzled at the sight of a horse who was out that day in a little conditions race at somewhere like Nottingham, a horse that was different class to all the others. 'Well that,' I said to my companion, 'is Thrown In.'

'Do you know that you say that all the time?' he asked, rather wearily. 'Two or three times a week, anyway.'

And I realised that, perhaps two or three times a week, you would indeed find a horse that was utterly Thrown In, a horse that was being given an easy little prep race, or a nice little confidence-booster. These horses were not in handicaps, they did not demand the maths 'A' level, they just had to be known about and noticed.

Nor, of course, were they backable as such, not on their own. But – and here the foundation stone of my system began to be laid – they could be backed in a kind of sequence: today, I would gamble on my Thrown In horse. Then I would wait, in smug certainty, for the next Thrown In to come along, on which I would gamble my winnings.

Then I would do it again; then once more; and so I would build a tall, strong edifice of accumulated money, which I would scoop up, kiss and put away, before starting all over again.

So I started it there and then. I went down to the betting shop, to see the first

Thrown In horse win by about three casual lengths, and to witness the birth of my theory beneath the bright Newmarket skies.

The bookmaker smiled as I picked up my admittedly pathetic return. Little did he know, I thought, that here was no foolish female backer, but a woman with a system. I began to plan how I would get my bets on. Obviously this would be difficult for a gambler who never lost.

And the system worked, truly it did, for five glorious weeks, taking me to the fourth and final leg of my Thrown In accumulator; when, with theatrical inevitability, it came a resounding great cropper.

A horse called Vacamonte – never to be forgotten – brought the carefully built-up edifice of my theory tumbling to the ground. He was one of Henry Cecil's bright young boys; what I hadn't known was that Henry's horses were starting to run under a cloud so heavy that not even Slip Anchor in a Class E handicap would have deserved a place in my system.

And so Thrown In Theory had succumbed, as all systems do, to the appalling unpredictability of horseracing. How could it not? But for those few brief, beautiful weeks, I had believed in it utterly.

I still do believe in it, actually. Madness and science, science and madness.

---

**MIKE CATTERMOLE** *got his grounding with Timeform and is now a regular on our TV screens, presenting for Channel 4 and Attheraces. Along the way, he's worked as a racecourse commentator and as a journalist, initially for the* Sporting Life *and currently for* Raceform On Saturday.

## Ante-post? Give Me a Break!

'OH, you work in racing, how interesting. And do you know that fat chap with the whiskers on the telly?' Yes. But apart from that, I really do appreciate what a lucky so-and-so I am to be doing what I am doing. As far as the punting goes, though, well let's just say it's been a bit of a rollercoaster ride over the years.

It had all started so well, too, when, inspired by my father, I staked a shilling – or was it 5p then? – each-way on Sovereign Bill to win the 1972 Lincoln. When you start with a winner at the age of ten, there's no going back.

We have had other triumphs. I recall Dad picking out King Con to win the Scottish National at 33-1.

The story goes that he was sitting at home watching the race on the telly trying to suppress his glee as Mum looked on, only feet away. I'm sure you know what it's like.

Dabbles in the ante-post markets have proved, er, somewhat character-building, particularly when you find the best horse in the field and it fails to finish first. Oh yes, we do that very well. Browne's Gazette in the 1985 Champion Hurdle was Dad's finest hour. He had a 16-1 voucher burning a hole in his pocket when the great horse lined up on the day as 'evens' favourite. What happened next defied belief. Dermot Browne lost control of his mount's head and the pair veered off to the left at the precise moment when the tapes rose, sacrificing the best part of twenty lengths.

I was sitting in the Timeform offices, watching in horror. If the Jockey Club ever get hold of Dermot Browne, do let my Dad know.

I had a bit of luck in the Champion Hurdle a little later, however, snapping up a bit of 25-1 about Celtic Shot. My confidence evaporated after he had been thumped by Celtic Chief at Sandown, and I then told all my non-racing mates to lump on the Chief at Cheltenham. It was with mixed feelings that I watched as Celtic Shot duly reversed the form on the big day, making me quids in but, at the same time, friendless and now regarded as the worst judge in the business.

Speaking of Celtics, let me tell you about Celtic Swing. Having seen him smash the course record at Ascot and leaving a horse called Singspiel trailing in his wake, I backed him there and then for both the Guineas and the Derby at prices between 20-1 and 25-1. He ended up being beaten in the Guineas – albeit narrowly – and went on to miss the Derby and win the French version instead.

This is also the same man who backed Cape Verdi over the winter for the Oaks – before she won the Guineas and then got re-routed to the Derby. I have also backed See More Business for the Gold Cup – the year he was carried out – and Cool Ground for the same race – the year he ran fourth, twelve months before he won at 25-1.

Oh, I had a nice touch on Lochsong in the Stewards' Cup. Having booked the ride for Willie Carson in my agenting days, I availed myself of some 16-1. Sadly, the bookmaker with whom I had the bet did a runner. Thomas Ashley was the name of the firm. If you ever come across them, they owe me about £800.

I should be so lucky!

**Sir Clement Freud**'s long career in the public eye has often featured racehorses, most famously when he rode a televised winner at Haydock in the 1970s. A full account of his involvement with the turf is given in his autobiography Freud Ego (BBC Books).

# Getting Away With It

I started gambling at the age of eight, at a bent roulette table in my Devon boarding school. Prior to that I had had no experience of money, for ours was not a household in which children bought sweets or were dispatched to get penn'orths of chips.

Then suddenly, in those salad days of pre-puberty, I received a weekly stipend of sixpence.

I read the *Sporting Times* in the school library, wallowed in the racing terms and longed for the day that ponies and monkeys would become part of my lifestyle. In Walberswick on the Suffolk coast, where my parents had a holiday house, I studied the runners and riders in my father's *News Chronicle*.

Mr Rogers ran the village garage and took bets, illegally, at his back door. Racing results were announced after the six o'clock evening news; one had to await the next day's papers to get the odds. My first big winner came in at 13-2. Oh, the joy of knowing you had backed a winner – and the wondrous wait to learn the extent of the coup.

Rogers was a miserable old sod who called me 'buoy', which is Suffick for 'boy'. Once, when a tuppence each-way bet came up and I had raced to his door to collect, he looked at me over his glasses and asked: 'How old are you, buoy?' I told him I was about a day older than when he had taken my money.

The cause of Mr Rogers' wretchedness was the first Wednesday of June, 1932. On that day, the Walls' ice-cream man who came across each summer morning on the ferry from Southwold pushed his tricycle up the street, went into The Bell for an Adnam's ale and told the assembled company that his governor's horse would win the Derby. He then sold Snofrutes for one penny and choc-ices for twice that sum on the village green, adjourned to The Anchor for a second drink and repeated his information.

Rogers, wearing his 'garage' hat, had driven someone to the afternoon train at Ipswich station. On his return, his wife said: 'Good news – I've taken over 50 bets.' All were on April The Fifth, owned and trained by Tom Walls of ice-cream fame. Rogers never smiled again.

In the summer of 1949, I managed a North Devon seaside hotel, spent my day off at a bookmakers in Barnstaple, ate local shellfish, adopted rum and lime and ice and soda as my drink and stuck a bet.

Stuck a bet; three words which represent the most acute agony I had suffered, then years of nightmares. A customer of quality who had arrived with wife, children, chauffeur and nanny came to me one June afternoon and said; 'Freud, d'ye have a bookmaker?' I did.

He said: 'Put me £100 on Benny Lynch for the Gold Cup. You'll get 100-1.' The reason for the 100-1 was that Benny Lynch was Alycidon's pacemaker and, even at 100-1, a pacemaker is a plum bad bet. I put the £100 in my pocket – 20 crinkly white fivers, eight weeks' pay. Reward for being knowledgeable about racing, I told myself.

This was the pre-TV age and I listened to the race on the BBC Light programme. 'The pacemaker is in the lead,' said the laid-back commentator. Then, half a minute later: 'Benny Lynch is 15 lengths ahead and shows no sign of slowing down.' Shortly after that, he opined that 'the lead is down to 10 lengths but he doesn't look like getting caught'.

Ruin stared me in the face. £10,000 was 15 years' salary. For £10,000 you could buy a 200-acre farm in Suffolk. It was 20 times the average reason for jumping off Beachy Head. A trickle of ice-cold sweat ran down the back of my neck.

By the time Alycidon was declared the winner, I had ceased to care; had lost my bottle. I never spent 'winnings' with less enjoyment; I understood how Mr Rogers felt and forgave him his boorishness. I also decided to take gambling more seriously than I had.

Someone wrote that racing journalists who don't bet on horses should be ignored. I think that is sensible: the most readable writers are those activated to work by bookmakers' bills. I have tried very hard to achieve a ratio between the bets I make and the income I receive for writing about racing. The answer to my wife's, 'Did you have a good day?' is now only rarely, 'Wrote a good piece but lost six times the fee.'

*For over thirty years a regular contributor to the* Sporting Life *and the* Racing Post, **TONY MORRIS** *has written extensively about racing, gambling and, especially, bloodstock.*

## Winding Up for the Next Big Score

NOT many people know this, but the secret of successful betting was revealed as long ago as 1866 by an eminent professor of mathematics at Oxford University.

It wasn't your usual crackpot theory that might deliver an occasional dividend, but a sure-fire method which enabled the punter to win on every race. Think of it; no tedious form study, no concerns about the state of the ground or the draw. You just hand over your cash and, a few minutes later, get it back with interest. Each and every time.

You probably think that I am now about to give this guaranteed successful formula a belated second public airing, or at least direct you to its original source, so that you may peruse it for yourself and put it into practice. But you have another think coming.

No, the fact is that, since I discovered this potential route to riches some 30 years ago, I have been struggling to get my brain around it. A brain that 'achieved' a maths 'O' level mark of 7% is at a serious disadvantage when trying to deal with such matters, and if you imagine I'm going to allow others more proficient in the subject to unravel the mystery first, you are mistaken.

But if I'm lousy at maths, I can follow logic, and the logic about the professor's system is masterly. I know it has to work, and it should just be a case of learning how to match the numbers with the reasoning.

Of course, it may have crossed your mind that, if this system was made public in 1866, how is it that brighter mathematical brains than mine didn't grasp it and put every bookmaker out of business long ago? There are more bookies than ever now, and many more mug punters. True enough, so maybe it's not just hopeless 'O' level students who have failed to understand the professor's methodology. Perhaps there is something about it which makes its application difficult. It could be that those pesky bookmakers cottoned on first, and instituted safeguards against it; they're not noted for giving a sucker an even break.

Yet the fact remains that the guy who devised the system, and made it known in a letter to the *Sporting Times*, died a very rich man. Do you think he derived all his wealth from being Professor of Mathematics at Christ Church, Oxford? Academics don't get paid that much, you know.

No, I believe he must have made his system work. Surely the riches acquired by Professor Charles Lutwidge Dodgson couldn't have come from his sideline as a writer of children's stories under the name of Lewis Carroll?

Well, I shall be in Wonderland when I eventually fathom the Dodgson/Carroll methodology and set it to work for me. Meanwhile, I shall just have to make do with the plan advocated by another nineteenth-century sage, a trainer by the name of William I'Anson. This is one that's readily understood, easy to operate, and makes perfect sense. What's more, it works, as I know from personal experience.

I'Anson was a wise man as well as a notable trainer, the only trainer to saddle two Derby winners bred and owned by himself until Arthur Budgett emulated the feat. He had seen a lot of lives ruined by excessive gambling, witnessed the misery it caused to the families of those who committed such self-destruction. His advice to his son, who was himself to become a trainer, came as a homily in three parts, each a perfect example of common sense, and incontrovertible in its logic.

The old man's first point came bluntly: 'Don't bet.' There could really be no rational argument against that. It was a mug's game, in which the odds were stacked overwhelmingly in the bookmaker's favour. The punter may enjoy a stroke of luck, even a run of luck, from time to time, but in the long term there could only be losses.

But I'Anson knew all about temptation, had succumbed himself, and was aware that his son would be no different. Hence the second message of his sermon: 'If you must bet, bet big.' Again, the logic was powerful. Fooling around, betting small sums was stupid. It was habit-forming, with regular losses of small sums swiftly amounting to large losses, while the irregular returns from modest successful investments merely served to feed the habit. The punter should never think in terms of a maximum wager, but rather should set a high minimum – one high enough to represent a significant financial risk. Therein lay the deterrent to wagering folly.

By no means the least of I'Anson's maxims was the last: 'Bet biggest when the odds are longest.' The punter who can abide by the second rule, being so selective in his wagering that he restricts himself to near-certainties, can come out on top. Betting biggest on the long-shot near-certainty offers the prospect of a life-changing return.

Of course, getting to know the identity of a long-shot likely to deliver is no easy matter. But in only 40-odd years as a punter I've found two, and they did – temporarily, at least – improve my lifestyle, because I adopted the I'Anson motto and really lumped on.

Such a shame that I couldn't resist all those small losing bets, but I reckon I'm now due another big one. If I could just get the stake together.

*Three times a winner of the* Sporting Life's *Naps Table, with thirty years on the racing staff of* The Telegraph, **TONY STAFFORD** *has seen and done plenty of punting. Now the main columnist of* Raceform Update, *he is also the author of* The Little Black Racing Book.

## Getting it Right – Mostly

I was watching the television one day and saw an interview with Stuart Wheeler, boss of IG Index. One thing he said rang true. He reckoned that nobody wanted to hear someone else's hard luck stories, so he had always kept quiet about any misfortune he had when betting.

Well, it's alright for Stuart, one of the great benefactors of our times. However, what a blow it would be for the legion of mug punters around the country and, indeed, the world. Their honestly-held opinion, that, but for the fact that racing, jockeys, trainers, horses and the stewards are all crooked, they would be habitual winners, would no longer be acceptable.

When it comes down to it, we're all meant to be unlucky. And the older I get, the more I realise I'm congenitally unlucky. Indeed, but for the fact that I do sometimes get out of jail at the last instance, I could be the unluckiest punter on Earth.

I feel this is an opportune time to put in print, by way of a confession, a history of an event in the long-distant past, just after the opening of betting shops in the early 1960s.

At the time, I was 'studying' for my 'O' level exams by way of an odyssey around the greyhound tracks of London and some of the Home Counties race tracks.

Generally, afternoons were spent at Park Royal, Charlton, Stamford Bridge and other much-missed greyhound ovals. Always, as an Economics student (amazingly I did eventually get an 'A' at 'A' level), the danger was that, between the group of us, the cash would not be sufficient to run to a bus ticket.

One memorable hot summer afternoon, we trudged all the way back from Dagenham to East London, dropping off one by one in Mile End, Whitechapel and Bethnal Green, leaving me a solitary last three miles home to Clapton.

One Boxing Day a few years later, the same group of school friends, now, me apart, all at University, enjoyed a four-track bonanza. This encompassed thirty-two races, with thirteen at Clapton in the morning, six each at Walthamstow and Harringay, before getting to White City in time for the last seven there.

A few years later, I was to become (at age twenty-one) the *Greyhound Express*'s chief reporter, and covered in turn Clapton and White City. I could hardly have had a better apprenticeship.

Well, suffice to say, with three races left at White City, following a scenic railway day of winners, losers and taxi cabs, I was dead level. I proceeded to back the last three winners and we all went out for a nice, albeit very late, meal in the West End.

My schooldays included many visits to Ally Pally, down the road from the school playing fields in far-off Muswell Hill (the schoolmaster could never understand why I didn't go back on the school coach to Old Street).

Between school and newspapers, I spent a year in a bank across the road from Tottenham Hotspur's ground and used to bump into John Pratt, with whom I'd played cricket for London Boys' Clubs a couple of years before.

John did better at football than I did in the bank and it was a relief when a great cricket friend, the late Ken Willson of *The Daily Mail*, got me a job at the *Walthamstow Guardian*, his first paper, and my stop-off point before the *Greyhound Express*.

It was in the bank year that I had perhaps the luckiest bet of my life. In those days, we worked alternate Saturday mornings and, one freezing January, I was approaching Dalston on my way home, where I changed buses and could just see the top line of a betting shop board from my upstairs seat.

The legend 'Sandown' stood above the line of the shop window and it gave a previously sombre heart, sure, it thought, to be denied any betting opportunity, a lift. I searched in my pockets as I got off the bus, finding a couple of quid, so went into the shop to peruse the card which, it seemed, had unexpectedly beaten the elements.

Imagine my disappointment when I saw the rest of the board, saying 'abandoned' in big letters. But then I noticed a less familiar name, 'Mullingar', denoting a small Irish track, yet another no longer with us (like Ally Pally, Park Royal, New Cross, Charlton, Stamford Bridge and the rest).

Well, there was nothing for it. I put the whole £2 on unnamed favourites and watched the BBC's 'Grandstand' that afternoon in growing amazement as the first five all won, with a 4-1 clear favourite in a field of eight and a 3-1, as my memory tells me, among them.

In those days, before televisions in betting shops, there were commentaries on English racing but, from Ireland, just the odd show followed by silence and, eventually, a result. Before the 'off', the betting was 7-4 and 9-4 the first two in the market.

Unsurprisingly, when the result came, the favourite on the last show did not win, but the second-best did. After a long delay, the SP came in and the pair were returned 2-1 joint-favourites. I remember I drew the best part of £1,000. In the way of such stories, I remember getting home that night from Clapton dogs with about £50 of it.

On the other side, an earlier night at Clapton had had a better result. In the afternoon I had gone with my father in his car to Epsom and watched from the car park on the hill. He asked me to put 10 bob (50p) on the third-favourite in the Blue Riband Trial, but I thought the odds-on shot a certainty, so, unwisely as it proved, stuck the bet.

To sort that out, I decided to hock his binoculars, at the same time explaining away the delay in bringing the £3,5s by saying the binoculars were pinched and I had chased after the miscreant, but in vain.

To say that the atmosphere on the way home was strained would hardly be adequate, but I waited until he set off for his preferred evening at Hackney dogs, before going out myself, having borrowed a pound off my mother, to Clapton.

Here, the Houdini element kicked in. With four races left, I had one shilling and sixpence, a tanner short of the minimum Tote bet (10p now). One of the said school friends subbed me the sixpence and I managed to find the next winner (9-4), had the next forecast three times (dividend 10/6d), thirty bob on a 4-1 shot and the whole lot on a 3-1 winner in the last, collecting around £30.

I made my way to North London to redeem the binoculars before arriving with a present for mother and a story of a visit to Epsom police station, where I had discovered the binoculars had been handed in. I have often thought that, if the last dog had lost, my future might have been much less complicated, if slightly less interesting.

As for advice, I believe you either need to know a lot or next to nothing. They say hard work brings results, but given that so many people now have identical racing pictures in their homes, rather than the imagined pictures derived from form books and newspapers, there has to be more uniformity of opinion. More reason, therefore, to look for the contra view and oppose the obvious.

Too much study can be counter-productive. I have had my successes, like many other people, but, as the anecdotes above show, if you get involved with betting on racing, you should expect to experience the highs and lows of outrageous fortune.

---

*Devoted Southampton fan **IAN CARNABY** would have enough to worry about during most seasons without having to find the next winner as well. A veteran writer and broadcaster, he numbers the* Sporting Life, *the* Irish Field, *SIS, BBC Radio Sport and Sky among his many credits.*

## How to Get Out of Trouble

WHEN Zoman was beaten a short-head by Opera House at the Curragh in 1992, I thought it might be a good idea to find out what life was like a few yards back from the edge.

You could say I needed Zoman to win that day. If your biggest bets are the ones designed to get you out of trouble, there is a flaw in the overall plan. I use the word 'plan' loosely, of course.

The story of the American gambler who pauses outside a casino and says: 'Jeez, I hope I break even tonight: I could use the money' is probably apocryphal. Only other gamblers understand it, anyway. Never tell risque jokes in mixed company, and never have gambling conversations with non-gamblers. You may come across as a bit of a character, but no-one wants to change places.

Pulling back from the edge means fewer celebrations, fewer conversations with complete strangers. But '92 was a watershed year. The year I realised that five or six winners would have to appear on the same piece of paper for me to force a draw. And I was never really into accumulators.

1987 was rather different. That was the year quite a lot of people wanted me to work for them. Strange, really, but there we are. SIS and Extel, who were vying to broadcast pictures to the betting shops, needed a presenter; John Sanderson needed a marketing man, and the London Daily News needed a racing correspondent. So I chose Robert Maxwell and his brand new twenty-four-hour London paper, which was really going to give the Evening Standard something to think about. And probably did, for the five months it lasted.

I'd interviewed Maxwell a couple of times for the BBC, around the time he was trying to merge Oxford United and Reading. 'What do you think of the name Thames Valley Royals?' he said. 'Sounds like a big box of biscuits', I replied, so it was probably just as well he didn't know who he was getting for a racing correspondent.

Anyway, the London Daily News folded, the compensation took a while to come through, I owed two of the big four bookmakers a few bob, and Ken Oliver, who'd recruited me for the paper and is now with The Guardian, said we really ought to have a drink in Fleet Street. Good idea, I said. I was already due to see some former Extel colleagues in Finchley at lunchtime, and the day began to take shape.

Like most racing people, I was following the Steve Cauthen-Pat Eddery title race very closely. Nearly 15 years later, John Hanmer, Steve's agent, told me he'd backed his man quite heavily, as had others close to the camp. Perhaps that was why the American ended up riding in Edinburgh claimers in early November.

But I didn't think he could win on Infanta de Castile that afternoon. My one strength is the ability to differentiate between modest form and poor form, and I knew that the filly's recent placed run at Newbury – which guaranteed favouritism here – meant very little. Hopping Around, on the other hand, had been running well enough on the northern circuit and Chris Thornton had engaged Pat to ride him.

I reasoned that one of the firms would take £250 and the other £200, and both bets were struck at 7-2.

For some reason – part of the brain may have been gearing up for a long day – I went out of the Finchley pub and had another £50 on him in cash. I had no desire to hear the race. The Extel lads arrived, we had a few jars, they went away again. I sat there for quite a while, taking it as a bad sign that there was no telephone call to the pub – pre-mobile days, you see – though they'd have needed Yellow Pages for the number.

The bet itself was hardly my biggest, but both accounts would be clear. On the other hand, a thousand each would take some finding. I once walked all along the front from Brighton to Hove, trying to conjure up the kind of disappointment I'd feel if a horse had been beaten (which it had), so that it wouldn't be quite as bad when I knew for sure. It didn't work, though. And I still had to walk back.

Looking sideways at the screen from the betting office door, all I wanted to see was two words, not one. And there WERE two, and the first one began with 'H', and I couldn't recall any other H's in the race.

Finally, it could only be Hopping Around, and it was. And I'd never really spent time in Finchley before – The Flask in Hampstead and the Galtymore Dance Club in Cricklewood, yes, of course – but not Finchley. A fine borough, I must say, bathed in late autumn sunshine. I admired it all the way to Swiss Cottage, and then remembered the fifty in cash, and admired it all the way back.

One takes a taxi on such occasions, but Ken had gone by the time I reached the Cheshire Cheese. I can never quite recall the early evening on days like these, but obviously there was the Cheese followed by the White Swan in Fetter Lane when it was still one of the great Fleet Street watering holes. Indeed, it features prominently in Anne Robinson's autobiography.

Gamblers celebrate any sort of recovery. We lose ten units, win seven, and miraculously break even. The things we get right were always bound to happen, and the things we get wrong were bad luck or pilot error. 'The highway is for gamblers, better use your sense. Take what you have gathered from coincidence', as Bob Dylan sang.

Not that Hopping Around was a coincidence. Three days later he finished sixth in the November Handicap, so he must have been a good thing at Edinburgh. I remember him with great affection.

All that remained was a quiet spaghetti in Frith St and a game of blackjack in Charlie Chester's. I couldn't really lose, because the accounts were square and I only had £200 in cash on me. They're not all that keen when you look relaxed.

The £200 became £1,800, but they don't really like you nodding off, either, so they got me a taxi to the Astor Court behind the BBC, where I used to stay when I thought I'd end up presenting Grandstand.

I woke up the next morning with £50 notes all over the bed, which should happen to everyone at least once. I can't remember what happened after that, but no doubt I found a way of giving some back. The form book suggests as much.

*JULIAN WILSON served over thirty years as the face of BBC racecourse broadcasting before retiring in 1997. A successful owner and breeder, he is the author of several books, including his autobiography* Some You Win, *published by Harper Collins.*

## The Winning Way

THERE are two different approaches to betting on horseracing. One is to view it as a means to make money; the other is to treat it as a pleasant recreation during a day at the races.

I have always adopted the former approach, partly because in the olden days, if you worked for the BBC, you needed a private income, and partly because I hate losing.

It is vital to keep an accurate record of your investments. My records go back to August 1961.

In 1962 I had a losing year. I have not had one since.

The big difference between my betting then and now is that in those days I had far more bets. At that time, there was no betting tax. It was introduced in October 1966 and abolished in the autumn of 2001. It is very hard to win with 'over-rounds' of 10%-12%, added to paying 9% tax. It means that you have to be ahead of the enemy by at least 25%.

In 1964, I had the absurd number of 741 bets. I was 'behind' all year until September 3rd, but ended the year winning £970 (multiply that by fourteen for today's equivalent).

That year I was 'resting' (unemployed) and much pre-occupied with the opposite sex. It was thoroughly unprofessional.

In 1966, I was employed by the BBC and reduced my number of bets to 255. That year I won £3,110. Since then, I like to think that I have been fairly disciplined. In 2001 I had 323 bets, but there is far more racing nowadays than in the 1960s.

My best year ever was 1992, when I had 340 bets. The figure does not vary very much from year to year. Of course, the vast majority are 'on course'.

Racehorse trainers who make money betting have far, far fewer bets. Almost without exception, they have no interest in horses outside of their own stable.

The art of making betting pay is hard work combined with a mathematical brain. It is all-important to calculate 'over-round' in a matter of seconds. Every punter will back winners and losers. The secret of winning is by backing your winners at over the odds.

Once you have 'handicapped' a race, you should evaluate the realistic percentage chance of each possible winning contender. This should be done overnight.

If you assess the favourite as having a 45% winning chance, but think he will probably win, any price upwards of 6-4 is appealing. Odds of 6-4 represent a 40% chance of winning, so you have 5% in your favour.

If you back the horse at 2-1, you have almost 12% in your favour. This is when you should bet.

The margin of 'over-rounds' in Britain remains fairly attractive, although they have increased since the abolition of betting tax. They compare very favourably with markets in South Africa, where very often they bet 50% in the bookmaker's favour.

The small punter has the great advantage nowadays of being able to compare ring prices with current Tote indications, and can bet accordingly. This comparison does not help substantial punters, because most Tote pools are so relatively small that they can be influenced by a single bet.

Ante-post betting remains the best opportunity for a substantial win. Of course, insider knowledge is extremely helpful, but the Classic horses are on show for all to see. It doesn't help when several good horses are housed in the same stable. That is where mind games come into play. The punter must get inside the owner or trainer's mind, and anticipate the decision that he will eventually make.

Spread betting is dangerous and, in my opinion, damaging to the sport. It is far too easy nowadays to benefit from a horse running badly. In the olden days, it could only be done in collaboration with a dishonest bookmaker.

Against the punter nowadays is the fact that odds-makers are extremely well informed. Gone are the days when betting forecasts were compiled by office juniors. Nowadays, the *Racing Post* betting forecasts are based on the bookmakers' overnight 'tissue', and correspond closely to the 'morning prices'.

Despite the helpful information freely available to punters, and the abolition of tax, it is no easier to win than ever it was. In fact, quite the reverse.

All-Weather racing is a negative element; there is far too much racing; and the quality of stable staff, with only few exceptions, is at its lowest-ever level.

Every week, several horses run unaccountably below form. The one factor that remains in the punter's favour is that he is never obliged to bet. Be professional; be selective; take *Raceform*; and burn the midnight oil.

Never drink and bet, and never take under the odds you have assessed. Bet mostly between May and September (when the going is relatively constant), and never chase losses.

If you have the self-discipline, and the will-to-win, you have a chance.

# CHAPTER 14
# TOTE BETTING

*An introduction to Tote betting
by **PETER JONES**, Tote Chairman*

## Diving into the Pool

ON 2nd July 1929, the Tote made its first appearance on British racecourses at Newmarket and Carlisle.

The system of pool betting, whereby money is amassed in a central pot and divided out between winners, was first established in France in 1872 by the formation of the Pari-Mutuel. The Jockey Club in this country saw this form of wagering as a means whereby betting could make a financial contribution to the sport.

Today, despite operating as one of the key players in what has become an incredibly competitive market, the Tote has never lost sight of the principles on which it was founded and continues to plough its profits back into racing.

For many punters, 'pool' betting is the only way to place a bet. The variety of bets available, the value offered and the reassurance of betting into strong, transparent pools combine with the lure of big rollovers and numerous high-profile big winners, making Tote pool betting an easily accessible and highly popular way to have a punt.

Smart punters always keep an eye on the Tote screens, searching out the value which will inevitably be found in pool betting, particularly in the more popular betting races, such as big-field handicaps. Accounting for their 'Win' pool deduction, the Tote bet to an over-round of 119%, whereas it is not uncommon for bookmakers in the betting ring to run to 140% or more.

Runners from smaller stables, horses perceived to be a stable's second-string and those from stables further afield, these are the ones to keep an eye on, as punting patterns on the Tote will often see them starting at prices far bigger than those available in the betting ring.

Those who find picking a winner too tricky should keep an eye on the 'Place' pool, which is another way many shrewdies reap value from a Tote bet. Most bookmakers take each-way bets, but only with the Tote can you bet for a horse to be placed.

For punters who find just picking the winner too easy, the Tote offer the Exacta (first two in the correct order), and the Trifecta (first three in the correct order).

The Exacta in particular has proved the 'way forward' in forecast betting since it was introduced in January 2000, consistently wiping the floor with its betting shop cousin, the Computer Straight Forecast (CSF), which it beats on an average 62% of occasions, paying on average 62% more.

Perhaps the most impressive display to date came during an evening meeting at Windsor on 22 May 2000. In the 7.15 race, Richard Hills led the thirteen runners home on 33-1 outsider Star Cast, followed by the 4-1 chance Inca Star. Despite winning £153.27, punters who had landed the unlikely forecast on the CSF could be seen crying into their racecards when an Exacta dividend of £2,884.80 was announced, better by 1,782%!

The more exotic bets, such as the Placepot, the Jackpot and the Scoop6 are the pool bets which really set the pulse racing. The promise of massive returns to small stakes, often coupled with large rollovers, continue to capture the imagination of the betting public, with the Placepot boasting an average return of over £600 and the Jackpot and Scoop6 pools regularly exceeding £100,000.

Indeed, the biggest Jackpot pool ever reached was a whopping £2,050,651 at Exeter on the 22nd March 1995.

Pool betting continues to grow and the future is incredibly exciting. Over the last few years, UK punters have been able to bet into the pools at the big Irish race meetings and in 2002, for the first time, the money will also be flowing the other way across the Irish Sea, as 'common-pooling' really begins to build up momentum. Although small at the moment, the steps taken in common pooling could prove highly significant.

Just imagine, somewhere down the line we could see pools throughout the world linked together, with punters from the four corners of the globe betting into a single huge pot of money.

# Tote Betting – a Recipe for Success

Your basic ingredient is the *Racing Post*. Few punters have the time or experience to assess a race without racing's only daily paper – if you're taking on a six-race bet, don't even think of starting without it. It's a cake mix in lieu of fresh ingredients, comprising a welter of talent, paid to do your homework. Punters are better-informed now than ever before and the *Post* must take the credit.

## 'The Mix'

1. Divide the six designated races into handicaps and non-handicaps.
2. Note the six betting forecasts, considering any horses quoted at 5-2 or less as possible banker material.
3. Go through the summary of selections; the more horses tipped per race, the more open the contest. Pay attention to any nap or N.B. and the horses most tipped.
4. Peruse the 'Training Area' columns – Newmarket, the South, Lambourn, the North. Let the local work-watcher's preference guide you.
5. Go with horses, trainers, riders and tipsters in form; nothing succeeds like success. Be ruthless, fickle and totally heartless. When they're 'out', drop them, but be ready to readopt them when they regain the winning thread. Fidelity, punting-wise, will not pay your losses.
6. With time at a premium and if you lack the experience to evaluate the form pages, reading through the 'Spotlight' assessment of each runner is imperative; it gives far more insight into a race than you'll gain by just scanning the verdict. Respect the advice of their advisors, even if you chose to ignore it; they have their moments, many of them magical.

The above information can hopefully guide you into placing each contestant under one of four headings; 'banker', 'probable', 'possible' or 'no-hoper'.

I would need a minimum of 30%, preferably 40% 'no-hopers' to justify a bet. Dive into a pool with less than 30% deadwood and your chance of success plummets.

If possible, try to note the following before you bet; the state of the ground, the draw advantage (changed going and stalls-positioning can affect the draw bias), non-runners, early morning market movers and the current form of horses, trainers, riders, tipsters.

If A P McCoy is a furlong clear as the jumps favourite for Tote bets, it's L Dettori and K Fallon who dominate on the Flat. Remember, in all Tote betting, success for them will rarely beat the SP, especially on Saturdays and at big meetings. Instead, try to note up-and-coming apprentices as soon as possible, particularly when they're booked for outside rides in handicaps.

# THE SCOOP6

Decide how much you want to invest, either alone or as part of a syndicate.

This is the Tote's most speculative bet and, at £2 a throw, treat it accordingly. It's a Saturday fling with 'mad money' and, as with the lottery and the football pools, your aim should be to win as much as possible for as little as possible.

Unsure of the minimum odds against you? To find out, just take the SP odds of the six betting forecast favourites as an accumulator – i.e. the lowest odds of a winning line – 2-1, 3-1, 6-4, 7-2, 3-1, 5-4 = 1,214-1

As you are invited to find the winners of six of the most valuable and competitive events at two of Saturday's premier meetings, my prices err on the side of conservatism. Nonetheless, I like to know what I'm up against and so should you.

Don't feel intimidated by the 'Big Game' punters – they require a dividend in proportion to their stakes and pay a heavy price for failure.

On the other side of the coin, the chances of anyone netting a large dividend with a straight line or small perm appeared remote until recent results, which have thankfully proved otherwise, as common sense denotes this bet does not merit a full-scale onslaught.

The £2 stake favours no-one and, on that basis, is fair for all.

If it disallows the average player more than minimum cover, the obvious deterrent to copious investment is sudden death, with no consolation on the win part of the bet.

Love it or loathe it, never has a Tote pool attracted such media attention, aided and abetted by Channel 4, generating excitement from the pre-pubescent 'puddler' through the professional 'poolie' to the veteran 'permer'.

## Think Placepot

One of the great features of the Scoop6 is the consolation aspect; if you don't win the main bet, but get a horse placed in each leg, you win a 'place' dividend.

On the whole, these have proved satisfactory and the smaller player could certainly do worse than aim for this part of the bet, rather than shoot for the stars and lose consistently.

Your arrows could still hit six bullseyes and, indeed, if you're investing between £24 and £96 or more, try to include one outsider or untouted selection, but only with a definable reason for doing so. Even with favourites or second-favourites up, this 'Ticket Shredder' will see you halfway to paradise and on course for premature retirement.

Before you do bet, please check the non-runners. Best races for the good place dividend are those with fields of four, six or seven runners (note fields of five, eight and sixteen for a non-runner, which drastically alters the place winning frame).

Closely graded races with open betting and the majority of runners tipped at least once will see place tickets dwindle with alarming rapidity. When perming, it is preferable to spread your net on these events rather than on a sixteen-runner handicap, where a shock result would probably scupper your hopes, whereas, with a field of four to seven, you have a sporting chance with half the runners covered.

Don't feel with this simple approach you will be just one of a crowd; on a 'gettable' scoop (a rare occurrence) you can win several times if your perm is on cue.

With unforeseeable results, most of the large perms will be in intensive care after just one shock and unable to accommodate a further 'unwanted guest'.

Play 'safe' and give yourself a chance of building up a useful Scoop6 bank, providing the ammunition for a more concentrated attack on a propitious looking card. It should be easier in midsummer but, with watering maintaining sizeable fields and with sponsored handicaps to contend with, the odds are stacked in favour of Tote House rolling up their pools for weeks at a time.

## Baking the Cake

Which is to say – perming, or, more to the point, cut-price perming. This is the only viable option for the average 'scooper', without access to deep reserves of cash or the massed wealth of a syndicate.

Even if you're staking between £36 and £48, you'll be looking for two to four bankers with a maximum of two to four selections in the other races. With a fixed stake of £2 per line, just see how the cost stacks up . . .

Two Bankers – 2 x 2 x 1 x 2 x 2 x 1 = 16 lines, costing £32.

Three Bankers – 1 x 3 x 1 x 3 x 2 x 1 = 18 lines, costing £36.

Four Bankers – 1 x 1 x 4 x 4 x 1 x 1 = 16 lines, costing £32.

This is basic perming, but sound if you're decisive. If you get a day when you're frankly undecided regarding your selections, 'cross-bankering' and internal reduction will give you wider scope for similar stakes.

## Cross-bankering

You've picked out four bankers. The remaining two races, featuring fields of eight and nine runners, are a puzzle. You don't want to leave out any of the runners, but the cost of including them all will be high;

1 x 8 x 1 x 9 x 1 x 1 = 72 lines, costing you £144.

That's tantamount to a £72 each-way accumulator on 4 horses – but my cross-bankering method will allow you to reduce the cost, maximising your winning chance for the funds available.

First, select one preferred runner from each of the two races. Then, make two bets; in one, cover the field in the first tricky race, whilst making your preferred runner in the second tricky race your sole selection, alongside your four bankers. Then swap things round for the second bet; cover the field in the second of the difficult heats (less your selection, which is already covered) with your bankers and your preferred runner from the first.

First bet – *1 x 8 x 1 x 1 x 1 x 1 = 8 bets, costing £16*
Second bet – *1 x 1 x 1 x 8 x 1 x 1 = 8 bets, costing £16*

Instead of £144, your two bets cost you £32. If your four bankers go in, along with one of your preferred selections in the difficult races, you win.

This is like a pools plan, with 'guarantees' catering for wide coverage at a greatly reduced outlay. This concept can be adapted to suit both perm and pocket.

Now let's say you've got a bit more money to spend. You've marked out three bankers, leaving you with fields of five, eight and ten to contend with.

You're determined to fully cover the five-horse race (after all, races with small fields can often be run at a false pace, setting things up for a surprise result). Making a preferred choice in the eight and ten-runner races will allow you to make the following perms;

*1 x 5 x 8 x 1 x 1 x 1 = 40 bets, costing £80.*
*1 x 5 x 1 x 1 x 9 x 1 = 45 bets, costing £90.*

Using these perms together, you cover your options at a cost of £170. However, had you simply covered the fields in the three races about which you were unsure, your bet would have been;

*1 x 5 x 8 x 1 x 10 x 1 = 400 bets, costing £800!*

At £170, we've probably moved into syndicate territory, but this example still shows how a perm can be substantially reduced, no matter how large it may at first appear.

## Internal Reduction

You have your four bankers, leaving fields of five and twelve to unscramble. If you can settle on two preferences in each contest, you might then try this;

*1 x 5 x 1 x 1 x 2 x 1 = 10 bets, costing £20.*
*1 x 2 x 1 x 1 x 10 x 1 = 20 bets = £40*

Again, you have two bets. In each, you perm the entire field in one of the two difficult races with your two preferences in the other. The combined bets cost you £60, half of what a full perm would have cost;

*1 x 5 x 1 x 1 x 12 x 1 = 60 bets = £120*

Your perm guarantees that, if one of your two preferences scores in either race (with your bankers also winning, of course), then you win.

## Scoop6 Bankers

My definition of the genuine equine banker is this – a horse that, barring accidents, will win, having ground, distance, weight, current form and the form of both trainer and rider all running in one's favour.

Nearly all of my bankers fall within a very narrow range of race-types. I like novice hurdles and, on the Flat, three-year-old maidens from May onwards (or mid-May if the ground remains good or faster), together with juvenile events after Royal Ascot.

Unfortunately, these races rarely feature in the Scoop6 bet. Accordingly, since we're forced to rely on only one horse in some legs of the bet, we have to be a bit more flexible about what we call a 'banker' for the purposes of this bet.

It helps if you can scan a card and pick out the 'soft' race – one in which, regardless of the number of runners, there are only a handful with real winning chances.

## A Favourite's Chance?

As with the Jackpot and Placepot, you can nominate the favourite as a selection. Whichever horse is returned favourite becomes your selection.

On occasion, this can be both plausible and inspired. This ploy can be used in races dominated by unknown quantity and during the early months of the season, when reliable form is thin on the ground and professional paddock inspection can cause market fluctuation.

As favourites fare much better in non-handicaps, while the Scoop6 card generally includes at least four handicaps, favourites have a low scoring rate in this bet.

However, if you're unable to choose between two or three of the market leaders and you're limited to one selection, picking the favourite is not a bad decision.

I'm a great advocate of choosing the 'fav' for Placepot and Jackpot purposes and have used it in the past to suit various methods of perming. Here are a few suggestions;

1 Make the favourite your sole selection, or banker, in the non-handicaps, whilst giving yourself plenty of cover in the handicaps.

2 Select the favourite in all six races, alongside your strongest fancies. With two selections in each race, that makes a total of 64 lines.

3 Selecting the favourite can also be used in the kind of cross-bankering and internal reduction I outlined above.

For instance, if you have four banker selections, leaving two difficult races of ten and nine runners, giving yourself the field in those races will be expensive, necessitating ninety lines at a cost of £180.

The alternative is to cover the field in one race, whilst going with the favourite in the other. You can then put on an identical bet, but switching races, covering the field in the second tricky contest while choosing the favourite in the first;

$1 \times 10 \times 1 \times 1 \times 1 \times F = 10$ bets costing £20

$1 \times F \times 1 \times 1 \times 1 \times 9 = 9$ bets costing £18

Your total cost is £38, a deal more manageable than £180.

Your guarantee is that, if your bankers go in and a favourite obliges in one of the other races, you win. If both favourites win, you win both bets.

Internal reduction can be applied as before. If, from those fields of ten and nine, you were able to eliminate five and three runners, respectively, leaving you with five and six to cover, your perms become;

*1 x 5 x 1 x 1 x F X 1 = 5 lines, costing £10*

*1 x F x 1 x1 x 6 x 1 = 6 lines, costing £12*

The total cost of your two perms is £22, rather than the £60 needed to cover a full perm, with the additional bonus of a 'favourite' obliging, which had been discarded from your original selections.

## Covering Against One Banker Losing

This is strictly one for the larger syndicates. The idea is to guard against the possibility of having got everything right, but to lose because one banker lets you down.

Let's take the following example. You have four bankers in fields of eight, nine, ten and nine. In the other two legs, you have two and three selections.

Your original perm would be;

*1 x 2 x 1 x 3 x 1 x 1 = 6 lines, costing £12*

In order to allow for one defeated banker, do these four perms instead;

*8 x 2 x 1 x 3 x 1 x 1 = 48 lines, costing £96*

*1 x 2 x 9 x 3 x 1 x 1 = 54 lines, costing £108*

*1 x 2 x 1 x 3 x 10 x 1 = 60 lines, costing £120*

*1 x 2 x 1 x 3 x 1 x 9 = 54 lines, costing £108*

What you're doing in each case is perming three bankers with your selections from the second and fourth legs and the entire field in the race featuring your fourth banker.

The total cost in this case would be £432, pretty hefty for a single bet. Then again, a full perm of the fields in those four races, together with your selections in the other two, would come to nearly 38,880 lines, costing you £77,760!

A little thought and judicious perming can be adapted to suit any stake.

## Insurance

With no consolation on offer for the win part of the Scoop6, we can create our own insurance at a low premium.

My worst scenario would be – bankers up, perm down. Accordingly, I'd suggest that, when you're using three bankers, insure yourself against such disappointment by having a treble to a minimal stake on those bankers.

If you're using four bankers, combine them in four trebles and an accumulator.

Another poor situation in which to find yourself is that, having strung together four or five consecutive winners, you're let down, perhaps on the very last leg. You bow out with honour, but no financial reward for your endeavour.

It is possible to guard against this, too.

You could try perming your selections from the first four or five legs, as long as you have confidence in them, to about 5% of your Scoop6 stake.

If (perish the thought) your first leg should let you down, you could perm the remaining five in similar fashion. If the next one should miss the target as well, then it's time to call it a day, but at least you can be sure of having given it your best effort.

## The Icing on the Cake

If all goes very well indeed, you'll find yourself in the bonus pool for the following week.

My only advice to those getting this far is this; experience to date shows that, if there are any other punters also going for the bonus money, your best course will be to beg, steal or borrow their phone number and pool your ideas and tickets.

Those who group together – scoop together!

## TOTE JACKPOT

Initiated at Royal Ascot in 1966, this bet breathed life into the machine.

As it stands now, the Jackpot has a minimum guarantee of £10,000 with dividends declared to £1 and a minimum line cost of 10p. Tote Direct now offers punters everywhere the chance to bet into this pool, which can be tremendously popular with a big rollup on offer.

The most important feature of the modern pool is that it weighs heavily in favour of the 10p/25p punter – unless a big syndicate enters the fray, it's long odds against a single player scooping the lot with a £1 unit.

Perming many lines at £1 per line can see stakes escalate out of all proportion to the possible return, after the Tote's take-out.

I haven't heard anyone claiming to make a regular profit from the Jackpot, probably because the day's toughest card is always selected as the venue for the bet. Even so, the bet cannot compete with the football Pools in terms of dividend.

My suggestion, with the aim of increasing both the bet's popularity and the pools on offer, would be to extend the bet to seven legs whenever possible.

Two of the bet's former features might also be revived – a consolation of 20% of the bet's daily take could be distributed among those who missed out by a single leg, while the Tote could offer a bonus to anyone with the single winning ticket.

The Tote might also generate more interest if they declared which meeting would host the bet some days in advance, rather than at the overnight stage. They might sometimes end up with a card that is not the day's hardest to solve, though it's usually pretty easy to forecast where that will be from one week to the next, but the gain would be that punters would have a bit more time to prepare for each Jackpot and more might become involved as a result.

Is there any value in this bet? Well, those with a bit of mathematical ability can use the estimated odds for their selections to calculate the return from an ordinary accumulator – if the likely return from the Jackpot pool will be greater, then that's your best chance of obtaining value.

## When to Play It

Freak dividends abound in pool betting – this is a rough guide to those occasions most likely to produce a decent return.

Apart from the take-out, the most adverse effect of the Jackpot is the complete lack of choice. The Tote orders its punters to find the first six winners on their chosen card, so it's up to you to decide when the mandatory card offers most appeal.

To justify a bet, you'll have to be satisfied that you can find every winner using a perm within your means, and also that the return is likely to be better than you could obtain from an accumulator to the same stake.

For the last criteria to be fulfilled, it will help if there has been a rollover. Once this happens, punters who wouldn't normally play the bet get drawn in by the prospect of a sizeable pot, so the money on offer can increase exponentially over just a few days. As is so often the case, patience and observation rule. Sooner or later, through no fault of the Tote's, the daily Jackpot will fall on a relatively simple card. Save up for this opportunity.

In midsummer, always watch out for a Jackpot card featuring small fields on a Monday or Tuesday. It could prove a lucrative bet, with little money running against you to share in the pool. With just the guaranteed £10,000 or a smallish carryover, you're unlikely to be competing with professional money or syndicates, who rarely enter the fray unless there's £50,000 or more up for grabs.

A few short-priced runners and a handful permed in from the handicaps may be all that you need to get a healthy dividend at many times the accumulated SP odds.

Perming ability is of the greatest importance – simply taking a few horses per race, more or less at random, will prove justifiably ruinous.

For my money, the best way is to rely on two bankers, have two selections in two other races and give yourself wider coverage in the remaining two races. If following this plan, please give yourself this protection – have a double on your bankers to cover your Jackpot stake. Nothing is more frustrating than to get your bankers up and lose money!

Don't be seduced into trying the Jackpot just because there's a big rollover – if it goes to an 'impossible' meeting, the SP could still upstage the dividend. If you fritter away on each Jackpot run-up, you'll have nothing in reserve for a concentrated attack on a propitious-looking card.

I don't advise pool betting on cards featuring more than one race of 'unknown quantities', like early-season maidens. When faced with such races, give priority to the horse offering the best public form and the SP favourite. If one of these races opens the card, you can wait until shortly before the 'off' to let the market guide you.

The two months immediately following Royal Ascot offer the best chance for Jackpot success on the Flat. The state of the ground is unlikely to vary much, there is plenty of recent form available, with large fields in the minority.

## Placing of Bankers

If you can, pick out bankers in the first half of the bet.

Most punters like to 'stay in the game' for as long as possible, so they give themselves plenty of coverage in the early races and tend to rely on bankers only in the last three legs. For this reason, Jackpot cards featuring three trappy heats followed by three fairly obvious winners tend to produce lower dividends than cards where the easier races come first.

This is also true for the Placepot and points value-seekers firmly towards those cards featuring tough races towards the bet's climax.

Don't just judge a race by the size of the field – a horse may still be a standout bet, even with fifteen rivals, while there are many five-runner events in which each contestant merits respect.

# Dos and Donts

1) When picking favourites, it's a great help to know which yards rarely get beaten in juvenile or maiden races when hosting hot favourites. With experience, you will get to know this. Equally, there are yards who can't win such races with unfancied types.

2) You must note and benefit from the effect of the draw in sprints. This should help you with a great many races through the summer, run on courses with proven advantages.

3) Don't bother with an each-way Jackpot/Placepot. Whilst success is entirely possible, these two bets require an entirely different approach. To use the same selections for both is the mug punter's easy way out, a method devised by the Tote to double your outlay and their turnover.

4) Don't be greedy about going in with big stakes – 10% of something is better than 100% of nothing. If a situation arises where you're unhappy leaving something out, include it and reduce your stake to accommodate the increased number of lines.

5) On the whole, it's better to be overcautious with the Jackpot. You may miss out on some good dividends, but the money saved through judicious abstention will more than compensate you for that.

## Jackpot Over the Jumps

Overall, it's far easier to analyse large fields of novice hurdlers for pool betting purposes. There is so much dead wood and, when something untoward does pop up, you can afford to miss out.

Avoid Jackpot meetings with big fields of handicap hurdlers, novice handicap and selling handicap hurdles and any card which incorporates the dreaded 'National Hunt Flat Race'.

Don't be swayed into Jackpotting at Cheltenham and Aintree come Festival time. Racing there has never been more competitive.

Syndicates and serious Jackpotters run scared and pools rarely swell in proportion to those at premier Flat fixtures, where cards offer more bankers and can appear less intimidating.

Use the novice hurdle for your base, while most handicap chases, especially those over three miles or more, can be narrowed down. Novice chases usually go either to those with the best exposed form or ex-hurdlers jumping the larger obstacles for the first time. The latter can often boost your dividend.

Experience is at a premium in novice hurdles and even more so in the junior division, where adept timber-topping can allow a horse to shrug off a penalty.

When a debutant with Flat form appears, it will not be an angel entertained unawares. Unlike an unraced juvenile, there will be Flat form as a guideline to its ability, distance and ground preferences.

The unknown quantity is the National Hunt Flat performer on its hurdling debut, taking on hurdlers with Flat form. Here, the market can mislead but, if you're able to include two selections, the exposed form horse plus the favourite should see you through.

From February, the tried and tested hunter chaser provides another possible banker. This sort is not as reliable a proposition as it was twenty years ago, but shocks in these races are few and far between and the ones at the top keep winning. Novice hunter chasers introduce the unknown and, unless you can get a point-to-point specialist to mark your card, you should steer clear.

You need a bit of a result to land the Flat Jackpot. The jumps equivalent is generally more straightforward and the occasions when you need to cover an entire field will be rarer. Nonetheless, opportunities to find value with this bet have dwindled.

## TOTE PLACEPOT

Deservedly the Tote's most popular innovation, the Placepot offers the chance of a good dividend for small stakes. It has three important advantages over the Jackpot;

1) The Jackpot is an 'all or nothing' bet and goes down with your banker. The effect isn't nearly so drastic if a Placepot banker runs a bit below your expectations. So long as it makes second (or third, if the field is large enough, sometimes even fourth), you'll go through to the following round.

2) A decent perm gives you the chance of winning the Placepot with more than one line, if you get more than one in the frame in the same race.

3) You can have a Placepot bet on the first six races at any meeting. Of course, this means rather more work on your part if you're going to sift through every card to find one that offers you an ideal winning chance.

## When to Play It

Self-discipline and restraint are imperative. Personally, I'd rather concentrate my efforts on just one or two meetings per month, though, as with most punting, there are no hard and fast rules.

At least if you're restrictive about when you play, you can be sure, when your arrows hit the target, that you're collecting winnings rather than recouping losses. Dive into too many pools and you'll drown.

If you're restrained about the occasions when you play, then, when you do enter the fray, you can afford to go a little over your limit.

What you're looking for is a card made up of big fields, which nonetheless feature few that can actually make the frame. Large numbers of runners tend to daunt the average Placepotter – his errors will hopefully increase the dividend available for you.

The reverse is also true. Look out for small but competitive fields, in which the favourite could easily miss the places. Many will view a favourite with few rivals as a banker, boosting your return if it goes down and you've pre-empted the situation.

While the Jackpot return can usually be forecast to a fair degree of accuracy, the Placepot returns often defy comprehension. It is in small pools at minor meetings that the freak dividends occur, needing possibly but one strange result to give you a dividend to savour.

The two best Placepot cards?

i) A straightforward card at a good meeting, when ground has been fairly constant for a few weeks, the form is working out well and there are few unknown quantities. You can eliminate with confidence and hope for more than one winning line.

ii) A midsummer card at a minor track serving up small fields of bad contestants. This can also occur at other times of the year when the ground is heavy, so that good animals aren't risked. You still have to find bankers but intensive coverage of several races brings its own rewards. An extensive perm to a minimum stake aiming at a big dividend should be your ambition in such circumstances. At this level, it's rare for the first two in the market to dominate in every race, yet most punters are betting with limited knowledge of most runners and so tend to rely on the market leaders. It might take just a single 'result' to give you a good return.

Cutting cost is essential to show a profit. The experienced Placepotter will be loath to cover the field if he can be sure that at least one runner is a no-hoper. Increasing the size of your perm to prolong your Placepot life rarely pays off.

## Dos and Donts

1) You **must** note non-runners before placing your bet. A non-runner taking the field from eight runners down to seven will mean that you have to get a horse in the first two in that race, rather than the first three. If there were five runners, reduced to four, then you'll have to find the winner! Moreover, if you're hoping that the favourites will miss the frame, thus building up a good dividend, then nothing is more frustrating than putting up a good-priced alternative that is, in fact, a non-runner. When that happens, your line ends up going onto the SP favourite – you've effectively thrown away your right to choose your own selections and, at the same time, lost all hope of a 'value' edge.

2) Broadly speaking, it's very hard to keep all the fancied runners out of the places on good or better ground at a top-class course. Perming them all, however, is sure to be unproductive. If you must stick to fancied horses, keep your perm small and play to a higher stake, so that at least you'll get a decent share of the easy pickings.

3) Don't be intimidated by big fields of handicappers with wide-open betting. Such races are anathema to the Jackpotter only. With these races, it's odds-on that at least one, probably more, of the first four home will have appeared at the head of the price lists that morning. This applies especially to sprints, where the following two pre-requisites apply;

   a) In races of five and six furlongs, stick to sprinters in form that have been consistently winning and making the frame. Sprinters can defy increasingly stern handicapping when in good heart but, conversely, cannot be relied on to take advantage of a dropping handicap mark if they're below par.

   b) Respect the effect of the draw and take into account what effect unusual ground conditions might have on the usual draw bias. If you're not sure how the bias will play out, give yourself at least one runner on each side of the track. Bear in mind that the effect of the draw is greatest in competitive races and may be greatly reduced in softer contests.

4) If there are eight runners or more, don't rely on unraced or unknown quantities,

or horses with no form. You shouldn't be clutching at straws – if you find yourself doing so, you shouldn't be Placepotting on that card.

5) Many big-field juvenile and maiden races can be safely covered with two selections at most – ideally, the SP favourite and the horse with the best public form. These criteria do not always point to the same horse; if they do, you've got two lines running onto a confident selection.

6) Keep an eye on the number of tickets continuing from leg to leg. This information is displayed in betting shops carrying Tote Direct, on the Tote screens at the track and on the racing pages of Ceefax and Teletext. If you find you're going into the last leg with two fancies giving you hope of a big profit, you may be able to give yourself a bit of cover. One possibility would be to put the remainder in forecasts to cover your stake at the least, in a small field. With 'cover' being my middle name, I rarely go for anything other than the first two favourites in the final leg, if I've been reaching for the sky in earlier races.

7) Don't go for doubtful stayers or horses from yards in poor form. The latter are unlikely to be persevered with if giving a below-par feel, while the former have an infuriating habit of fading out of the places.

It's still easier to do the Placepot in the last few months of the season than in the opening six weeks, when too many unknown, unfit and unfancied horses will hamper your aspirations. You may spend April and May itching with frustrated anticipation but at least in the summer you'll get the benefit of exposed form, which is levelling out, while improvers are easier to pinpoint.

Maidens and juveniles still pose a problem but those restricted to three-year-olds can be readily picked apart. You'll find many disappointing types being desperately dropped in class. These are dangerous vehicles for 'win' bets but offer a smooth ride for Placepot punters.

## Placepot Over the Jumps

Here again, bankers stem from novice and juvenile hurdles. With two or three places, horses with exposed current form can get turned over by unraced ex-Flat performers but, barring accidents, they should be hard to keep out of the frame.

Don't rely on any horse from a stable clearly out of form. Avoid dodgy jumpers and any hurdlers that are less then fluent, except in races with four runners or less. Experienced chasers and safe jumpers are suitable Placepot material, so long as ground, course and stable form are suitable – with no draw or stalls positions to worry about, it's the going and the obstacles that prove destructive.

Small fields at minor meetings on fast ground outside mid-season create many outsize dividends. Mediocre horses with obstacles to contend with are alarmingly likely to run below form, perhaps because connections have gone to the well once too often, or because they've got jarred up on the ground.

Much of the formula I've set out above for the Flat Placepot also holds true for the jumps. Many short-priced favourites are at false odds – these must be opposed, while a lack of consistency in the form at low levels over the jumps means you should spread your net at minimum stakes to guard against a shock result.

In chases, even more than in hurdles, note the bare form figures and steer clear of 'F', 'U' and 'P'. Those performers which seldom win but usually get placed and rarely fall should be running for you.

The unraced hurdler should be avoided as a banker, unless there's an extra place to fill, but the hurdler first time over fences must be included whenever possible, especially those with even a smattering of timber form, with a good trainer and rider.

With juvenile and novice hurdles, take the best public form as well as the SP favourite, if two selections are possible.

On testing ground, proven stamina and ability to act on it are essential Placepot elements. When unsure, favour those which will plod on over those which, on past form, are more likely to fade out of the frame.

On good ground before Cheltenham, at leading meetings, it's unusual to get big dividends. Form, on the whole, works out and it's only in the fields with seven runners or fewer that accidents, false-run races and close grading can conspire to result in more than a two-figure pay-off. Aim for small perms to higher stakes.

Even more important than on the Flat is that you're prepared to omit horses who've gone over the top or out of form. Even if such horses are clearly the best in terms of past form or speed figures, you must have the courage to look elsewhere.

The going can get tough in handicap hurdles, especially in low grades but at the higher levels, as on the Flat, the first line of any list of morning prices usually hosts at least one or two of the eventual principals.

Non-handicap sellers and claimers rarely see both first and second favourites unplaced.

The Placepot at the big jumps festivals can provide gigantic rewards but it's such a gamble that, if you're in form, you'll get home with a small perm to a modest stake. On the other hand, if you're out of form, you could lay out a large sum and still fail without honour.

Maximum Placepot stakes should be made on a card where you think you have an odds-on chance of six right, with a dividend to justify your outlay.

## TOTE QUADPOT – A SECOND BITE AT THE CHERRY

THE Placepot's kid brother has yet to set me on fire but pools are often respectable now, making this an interesting proposition from time to time.

Designed as a consolation for those knocked out in the first two legs of the Placepot, it also offers a fun alternative for those who choose not to invest as heavily as Placepot punters are generally required to. You get a chance to make more consistent, albeit limited, profits.

It has advantages over the Placepot. Most importantly, punters can watch the first two races to judge the state of the ground and the effect of the draw. They can take into account any late non-runners and make a final assessment of which yards have their horses in peak form and which are beginning to struggle.

Dividends may be smaller, but stakes are also reduced in proportion. Extensive coverage is neither necessary nor desirable unless there are two very tricky races to solve. Professional players will always be rare unless there's an especially large pool.

Otherwise, similar considerations apply to this bet as to the Placepot. The most important thing is to be careful in your choice of which cards to play.

If there are two obvious bankers in the opening races of the Placepot card you intend to play on, you could do a lot worse than joining the party after they have been run. If one or both fail to make the Placepot frame, you would have been sunk, and, if both are placed, you have missed little, dividend-wise, by watching and waiting.

This is an occasion from which you can only benefit, especially if you are a smaller player.

Also, if you are an infrequent or selective placepotter, you should enter the final four legs of your perm for the Quadpot if you have gone out on the first two races, but only if you had been confident that your perm was going to be successful in the first place.